Little Ones Sing Praise

Christian Songs
for Young Children

CONCORDIA PUBLISHING HOUSE • SAINT LOUIS

Copyright © 1989 Concordia Publishing House
3558 S. Jefferson Avenue, St. Louis, MO 63118-3968
Manufactured in the United States of America

All rights reserved. No part of this publication may be reproduced, stored in a retrieval system, or transmitted, in any form or by any means, electronic, mechanical, photocopying, recording or otherwise without the prior written permission of Concordia Publishing House.

Contents

Foreword 5

Hymns and Spiritual Songs
    Opening 7
    Prayer 13
    Prayer/Mealtime 16
    Wiggles Out 18
    Offering 22
    Daily Living 23
    Closing 39
    Jesus 41
    Scripture 48
    Praise and Thanksgiving 56
    Creation 72
    Advent 77
    Christmas 81
    Holy Week/Easter 92
    Baptism 97
    Witness 99
    Piggyback Songs 107

Acknowledgments 111

Topical Index 115

Index of First Lines and Common Titles 118

Foreword

Little Ones Sing Praise is a collection of songs to help young children as they pray, praise, and offer their thanks to God. Through singing they are also nurtured in the faith and have the opportunity to witness to one another. The songs in this collection have been selected primarily for children two to five years old.

The selections have been coded to identify the youngest age at which each is appropriate (3↑ = age 3 and up). The language and musical range were primary factors in determining age appropriateness.

Ideally, an adult will lead young children in singing without using musical accompaniment. This book, however, contains keyboard settings for those who desire this assistance. All settings have been designed to enable an individual with limited keyboard skills to accompany the songs. Many songs also include chords for guitar. The keyboard and guitar accompaniments are not designed to be played together; use either one or the other.

The selections in this collection provide resources for a variety of settings in Christian early childhood programs. Most are also appropriate for home use.

This new songbook is the result of more than two years of research, planning, collecting, and editing. Members of the committee were Marilynn Beccue, Martha Streufert Jander, and Arnold Schmidt of the Board for Parish Services of The Lutheran Church–Missouri Synod; Dorothy Schultz of Bronxville, New York, representing the Commission on Worship; and Barry Bobb of Concordia Publishing House.

Little Children, Sing to God! (Concordia, 1960) and *The Little Christian's Songbook* (Concordia, 1975) served as most useful resources for the committee as they prepared this volume. The committee wishes also to acknowledge the assistance of scores of early childhood teachers and consultants who contributed to its development, as well as the many children who submitted illustrations.

Little Ones Sing Praise is presented to the church with the prayer that it will bring glory to God and spiritual joy and growth to its users.

Notes to Leaders

What kinds of songs help to build the faith of children as they offer their praises to God? Following are some of the criteria used by the committee to select the contents of *Little Ones Sing Praise*:

1. Length of selections should be appropriate. Songs for two-year-olds must be very short; selections may be longer as children grow older. Selections also may be longer if they contain large amounts of repetition.

2. The melody should have a small range. In this book, most songs for two-year-olds have only a five-step range. Most of the songs have a range of no more than an octave.

3. For those teachers more comfortable working with only the folk tunes and nursery rhymes they know, a section of "piggyback" songs is included.

4. Young children enjoy participating in corporate worship. *Little Ones Sing Praise* contains segments of some hymns and liturgical pieces sung in the service.

Many familiar songs contain words, phrases, or concepts that young children cannot understand. Altered texts have been provided here for some of these songs.

Several of the selections in this collection will assist leaders in ministering more effectively to the diversity that exists in our society. These songs contain the words from another language or are signed for children with hearing disabilities.

Helping the out-of-tune singer is an everyday challenge for those who work with young children. It is a very important task, however, since some children will never find their true singing voice if not worked with individually or in class. The following two resources are highly recommended for teachers who desire to motivate and enable young children to sing well and gain satisfaction from this most personal of musical expressions:

- *Children Sing His Praise.* Edited by Donald Rotermund. Concordia Publishing House 99-1238. Chapters 3, 5.
- *Of Primary Importance.* By Helen Kemp. Choristers Guild CGBK-50. Chapters 1-2.

The developers of *Little Ones Sing Praise* urge leaders to use the selections and suggestions in this volume to help young children participate in the worship of their congregations–in the Sunday morning services, Sunday school, preschools, day-care centers, kindergartens, and other settings.

8 OPENING

Gathering Song

Dorothy N. Schultz   Dorothy N. Schultz

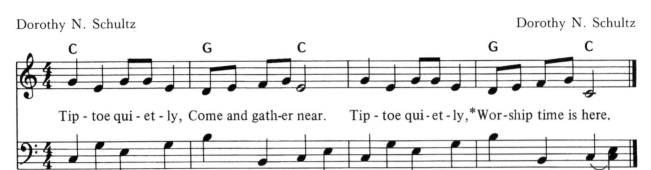

* Jesus time, story time, music time, cleanup time
Use this song to move children from one area or activity to another.

Good Morning

Traditional   Traditional

* Alternate key for guitar

OPENING 9

Happy Now We Gather

Mary L. Brummer J. C. Rinck

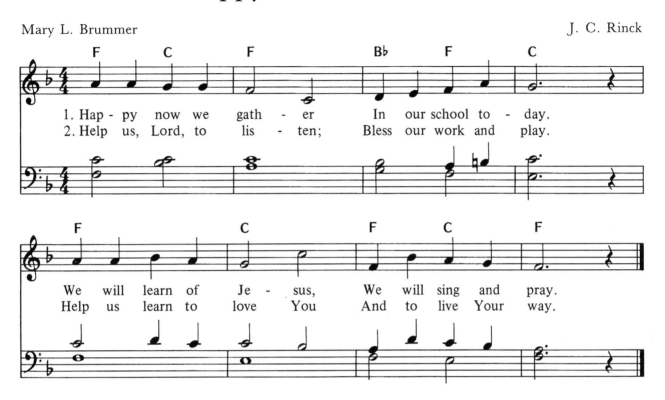

1. Hap-py now we gath-er, In our school to-day.
2. Help us, Lord, to lis-ten; Bless our work and play.

We will learn of Je - sus, We will sing and pray.
Help us learn to love You And to live Your way.

Hello, Hello! How Are You?

Kathleen Hurty Marie Pooler

1. Hel-lo, hel-lo! How are you? You are my friend and
2. *Kev-in, Kev-in, how are you? You are my friend and

I love you. Hel-lo, hel-lo! How are you? Je-sus loves me, He loves you.
I love you. *Laur-a, Laur-a, how are you? Je-sus loves me, He loves you.

* Insert names of children here.

I Have a Hello in My Heart

Jack Miffleton Jack Miffleton

3. I have a hello in my *lips,* and it's just for you;
   I have a hello in my lips, a hello *smile* for you.
   So hello from my lips,
     and hello from my eyes,
       and hello from my heart to you.

4. I have a hello in my *hands,* and it's just for you;
   I have a hello in my hands, a hello *shake* for you.
   So hello from my hands,
     and hello from my lips,
       and hello from my eyes,
         and hello from my heart to you.

5. I have a hello in my *arms,* and it's just for you;
   I have a hello in my arms, a hello *hug* for you.
   So hello from my arms,
     and hello from my hands,
       and hello from my lips,
         and hello from my eyes,
           and hello from my heart to you.

6. I have a hello in my *feet,* and it's just for you;
   I have a hello in my feet, a hello *hop* for you.
   So hello from my feet,
     and hello from my arms,
       and hello from my hands,
         and hello from my lips,
           and hello from my eyes,
             and hello from my heart to you.

Point to body parts as the song is sung. Children may choose body parts to create their own stanzas.

OPENING 11

I Like to Be in Sunday School

Our Church Family

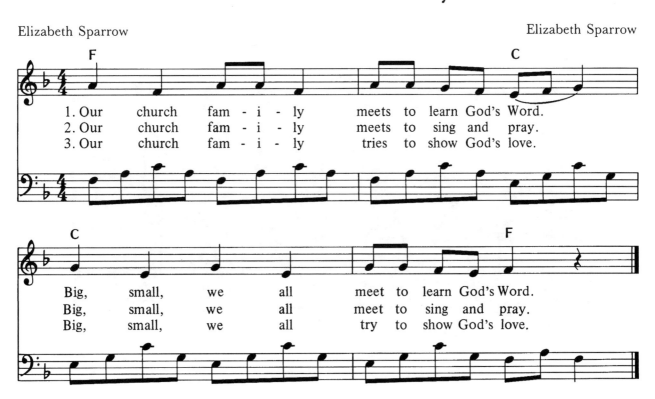

12 OPENING

We Are in God's House Today

Theodore G. Stelzer, 1892-1956

Orientis partibus
French, 13th cent.

4↑

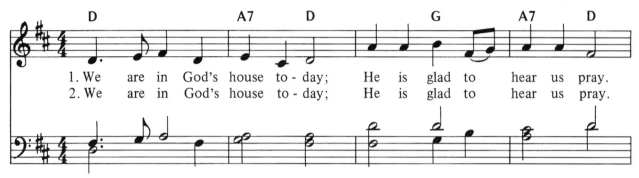

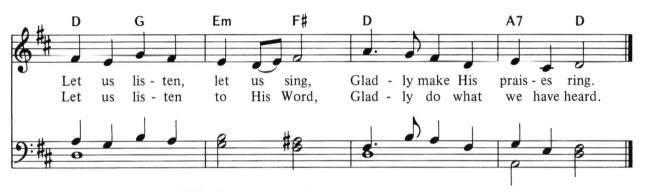

1. We are in God's house to-day; He is glad to hear us pray.
   Let us lis-ten, let us sing, Glad-ly make His prais-es ring.
2. We are in God's house to-day; He is glad to hear us pray.
   Let us lis-ten to His Word, Glad-ly do what we have heard.

For another Opening Song, see "Hello, Hello" on page 40.

PRAYER 13

Dear Father in Heaven

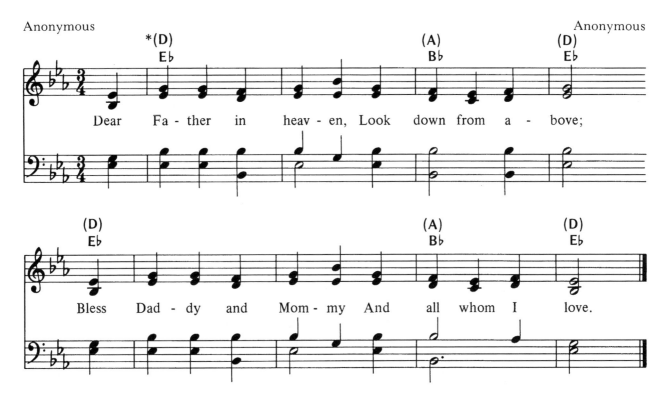

* Alternate key for guitar

Father, I Adore You

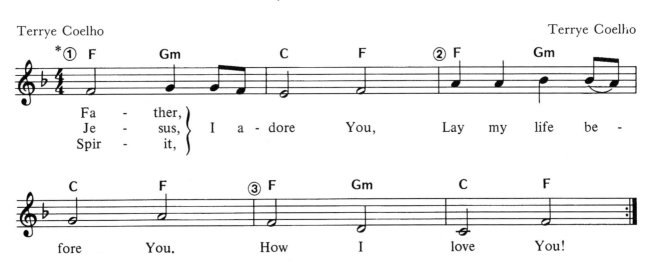

* May be sung as a round.
This can be a very calming song in preparation for worship.

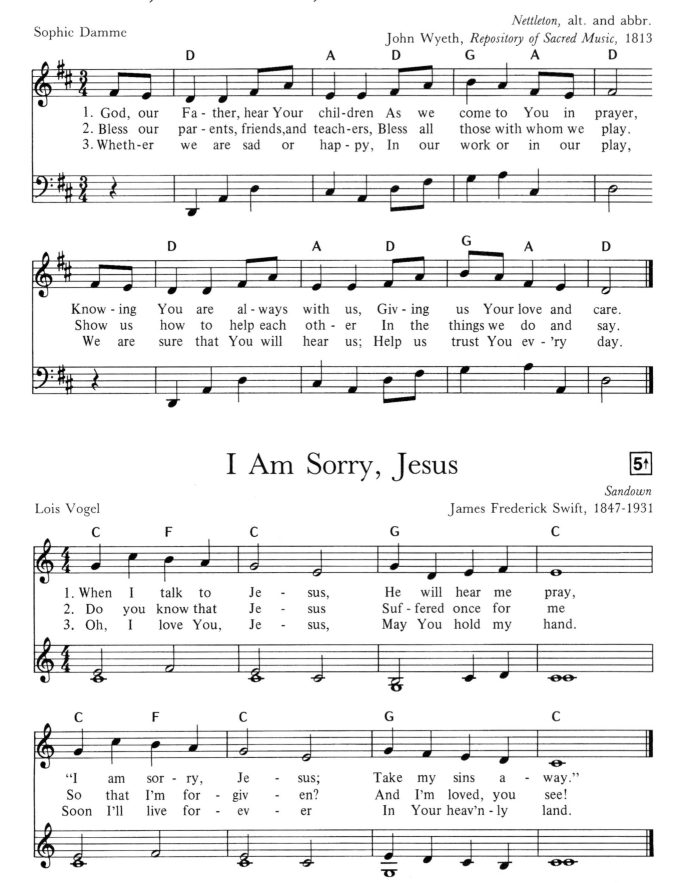

PRAYER 15

Jesus Listens When I Pray

Clara Ketelhut

Arthur W. Gross
Arr. by John C. Wohlfeil

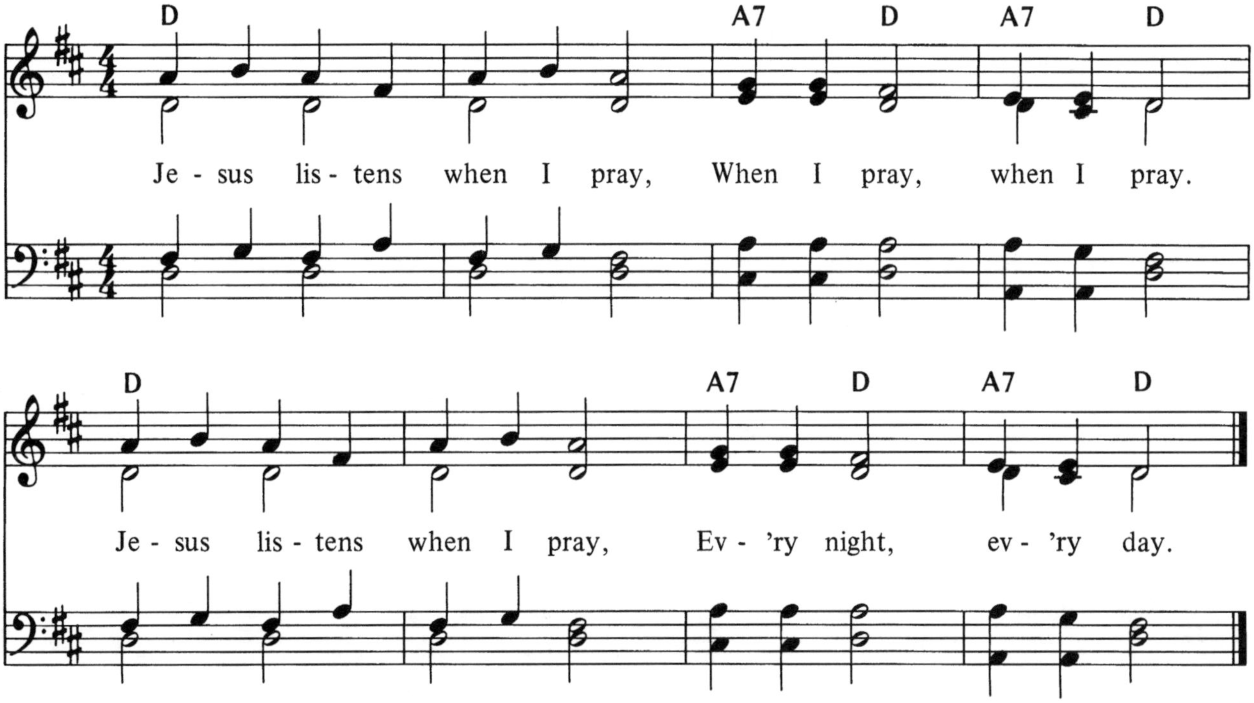

Je - sus lis - tens when I pray, When I pray, when I pray.

Je - sus lis - tens when I pray, Ev - 'ry night, ev - 'ry day.

We Pray for Each Other

O. William Luecke

O. William Luecke

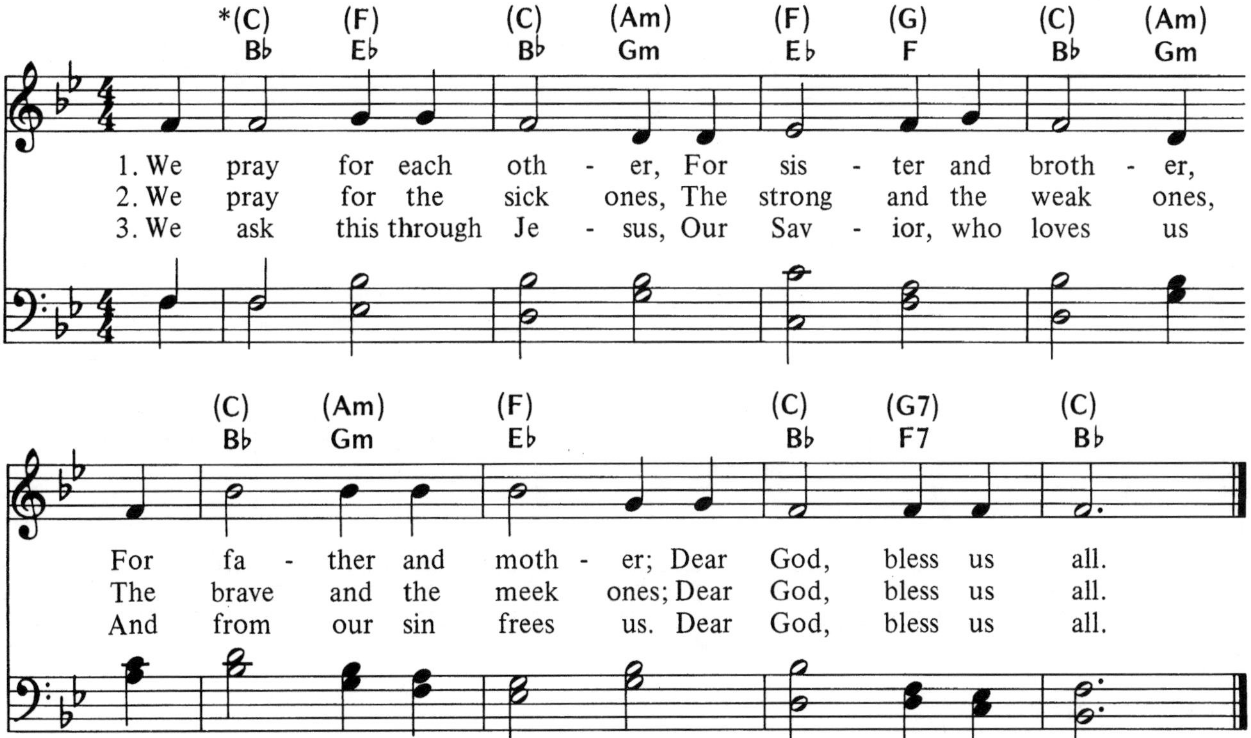

1. We pray for each oth - er, For sis - ter and broth - er,
2. We pray for the sick ones, The strong and the weak ones,
3. We ask this through Je - sus, Our Sav - ior, who loves us

For fa - ther and moth - er; Dear God, bless us all.
The brave and the meek ones; Dear God, bless us all.
And from our sin frees us. Dear God, bless us all.

* Alternate key for guitar

16 PRAYER/MEALTIME

The Lord Is Good to Me
(The Johnny Appleseed Song)

Kim Gannon and Walter Kent   Kim Gannon and Walter Kent

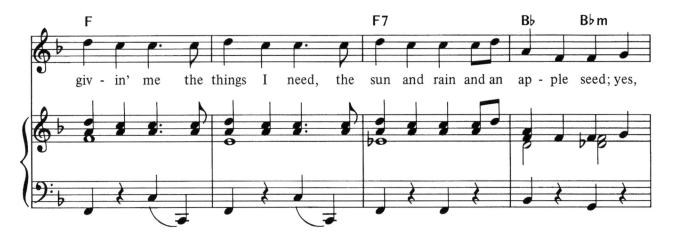

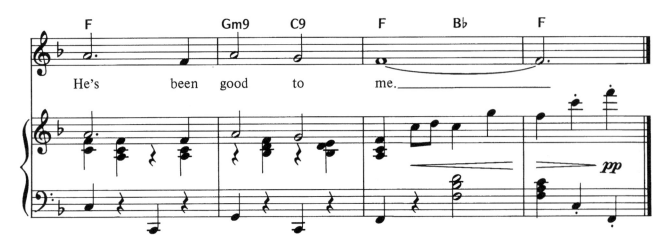

Sing this song as a meal-time prayer.

© 1946 Walt Disney Music Company. Copyright Renewed. Printed by Permission. All Rights Reserved.

PRAYER/MEALTIME 17

Our Hands We Fold

Anonymous
Theodore G. Stelzer, 1892-1956

Our hands we fold, our heads we bow; For food and drink we thank You now. A-men.
*Our hands we fold, our heads we bow; Our gifts, dear God, we give You now. A-men.

* Offering song

Thank You for the World So Sweet

Mrs. E. Rutter Leatham
Dorothy N. Schultz

Thank You for the world so sweet, Thank You for the food we eat,
Thank You for the birds that sing, Thank You, God, for ev-'ry-thing.

WIGGLES OUT 19

Chatter with the Angels

Spiritual

* *March* with the angels
 Skip with the angels
 Dance with the angels
 Tiptoe with the angels

Do the actions indicated in each stanza.

WIGGLES OUT 21

I Can Stamp

Gretchen Anderson

American folk song
Adapted by Gretchen Anderson

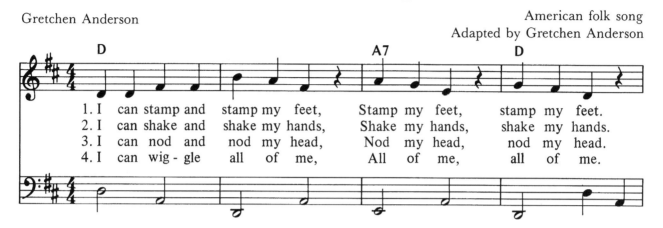

1. I can stamp and stamp my feet, Stamp my feet, stamp my feet.
2. I can shake and shake my hands, Shake my hands, shake my hands.
3. I can nod and nod my head, Nod my head, nod my head.
4. I can wig-gle all of me, All of me, all of me.

I can stamp and stamp my feet. God gave me these feet.
I can shake and shake my hands. God gave me these hands.
I can nod and nod my head. God gave me this head.
I can wig-gle all of me. God made all of me.

Let the children do the actions described.

22 OFFERING

Father, Bless the Gifts We Bring You

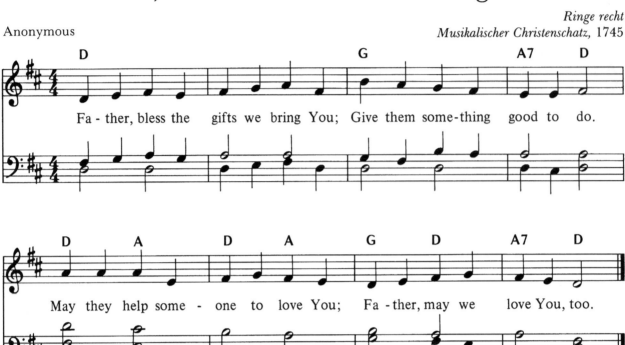

Since My Heavenly Father

For another Offering Song, see "Our Hands We Fold" on page 17.

Amigos de Cristo

John Ylvisaker   John Ylvisaker

This song introduces children to a few Spanish words. "Amigos de Cristo" means "friends of Christ."

DAILY LIVING 25

I Have a Friend

Unknown Traditional

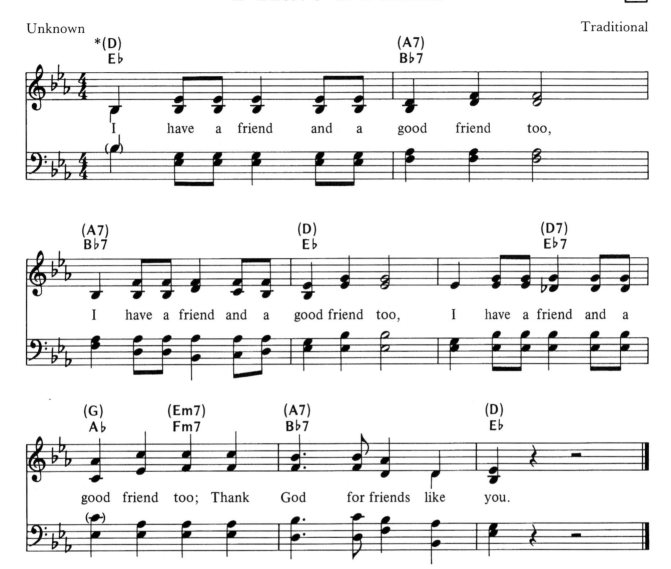

* Alternate key for guitar
Sing the song several times. Children point to a different friend each time on the word you.

I'm as Happy as Can Be

O. William Luecke
Arr. by John C. Wohlfeil

O. William Luecke

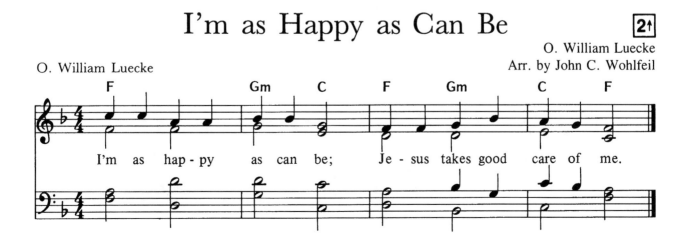

26 DAILY LIVING

God Has Sent His Angels Down

Martha Jander

Orientis partibus
French, 13th cent.

1. God has sent His angels down; They are with me, all a-round.
   Safe they keep me all the day, While I work and when I play.
2. God has sent His angels down; They are with me, all a-round.
   They pro-tect me through the night; Glad I wake with morn-ing light.

God Is Near

William A. Kramer

Franz Schubert, 1797-1828; adapt.

In our work and in our play God is with us ev-'ry day;
There-fore we will nev-er fear, For our lov-ing God is near.

DAILY LIVING 27

I'm Growing

Lois R. Brokering — Lois R. Brokering

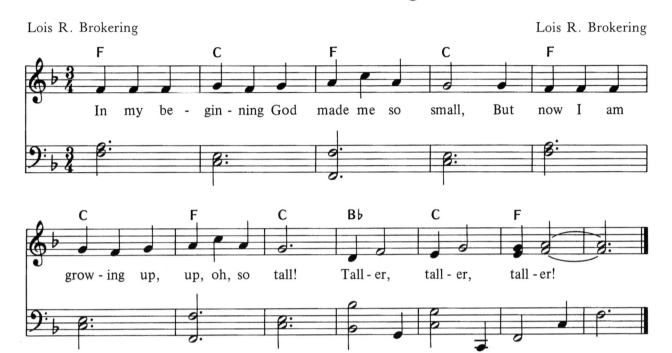

In my be-gin-ning God made me so small, But now I am grow-ing up, up, oh, so tall! Tall-er, tall-er, tall-er!

Hold your hands very close to the floor on "so small." Make them rise higher and higher to indicate growth, so that you are stretching up to the ceiling by the end of the song.

I'm Sorry

Lois R. Brokering — Lois R. Brokering

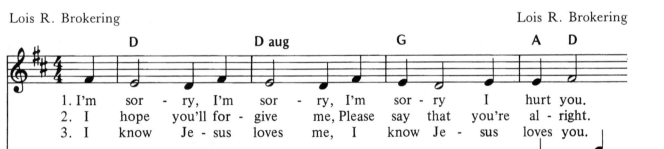

1. I'm sor-ry, I'm sor-ry, I'm sor-ry I hurt you.
2. I hope you'll for-give me, Please say that you're al-right.
3. I know Je-sus loves me, I know Je-sus loves you.

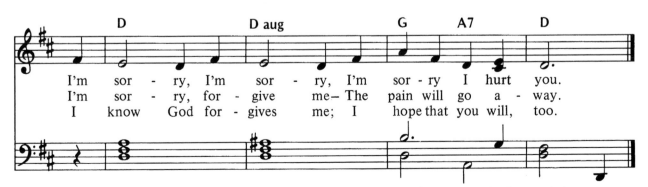

I'm sor-ry, I'm sor-ry, I'm sor-ry I hurt you.
I'm sor-ry, for-give me—The pain will go a-way.
I know God for-gives me; I hope that you will, too.

Use this song any time a misbehavior occurs, when confession and forgiveness are needed. Don't reserve it just for worship time.

I'm Glad

28 DAILY LIVING

Carol Greene
German folk tune

1. I'm glad you're you; I'm glad I'm me; I'm glad! I'm glad! God made us each so spe-cial-ly. I'm glad! I'm glad! I'm glad! I'm glad!
2. I've got my name; you've got your name; I'm glad! I'm glad! And still God loves us both the same. I'm glad! I'm glad! I'm glad! I'm glad!
3. I'm not like you; you're not like me; I'm glad! I'm glad! But such good friends we both can be. I'm glad! I'm glad! I'm glad! I'm glad!

The children might point to the appropriate persons while singing this song; they could also clap on the rests.

DAILY LIVING 29

I Have Hands

Margaret M. Self

Jeanne P. Boozer

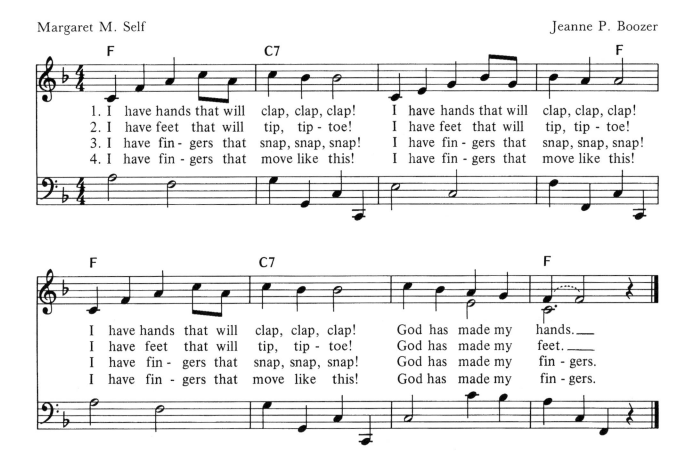

1. I have hands that will clap, clap, clap! I have hands that will clap, clap, clap!
2. I have feet that will tip, tip-toe! I have feet that will tip, tip-toe!
3. I have fingers that snap, snap, snap! I have fingers that snap, snap, snap!
4. I have fingers that move like this! I have fingers that move like this!

I have hands that will clap, clap, clap! God has made my hands.
I have feet that will tip, tip-toe! God has made my feet.
I have fingers that snap, snap, snap! God has made my fingers.
I have fingers that move like this! God has made my fingers.

5. I have knees that will bend like this!
6. I have hands that will be so still!
7. I have hands that will lock up tight!
8. I have arms that will reach up high!
9. I have lips that will (*whistle*)!

Let the children do the actions described.

Happy Birthday to You

Mildred and Patty Hill, st. 1
Unknown, st. 2

Traditional

1. Happy birthday to you,
   Happy birthday to you,
   Happy birthday, dear (*name*)
   Happy birthday to you!

2. May Jesus bless you,
   May Jesus bless you,
   May He guide you and keep you,
   May Jesus bless you.

St. 1 © 1935 SUMMY-BIRCHARD MUSIC (renewed). All rights reserved. Used by permission.

30 DAILY LIVING

God's a Father Kind and True

Arnold C. Mueller, 1891-1980, sts. 1-3,5
Unknown, st. 4

Theodore G. Stelzer, 1892-1950

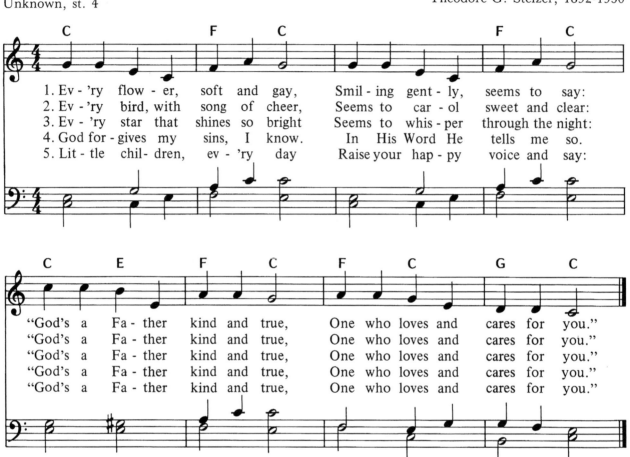

1. Ev-'ry flow-er, soft and gay, Smil-ing gent-ly, seems to say:
2. Ev-'ry bird, with song of cheer, Seems to car-ol sweet and clear:
3. Ev-'ry star that shines so bright Seems to whis-per through the night:
4. God for-gives my sins, I know. In His Word He tells me so.
5. Lit-tle chil-dren, ev-'ry day Raise your hap-py voice and say:

"God's a Fa-ther kind and true, One who loves and cares for you."

Let the children pretend to be flowers, birds, stars, and themselves with the appropriate stanzas.

Love, Love, Love

Lois and Herbert Brokering

Lois and Herbert Brokering

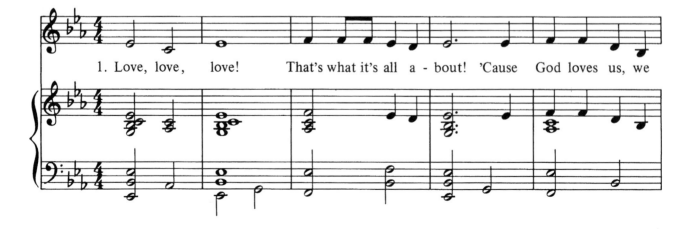

1. Love, love, love! That's what it's all a-bout! 'Cause God loves us, we

2. Peace, peace, peace! That's what it's all about!
3. Joy, joy, joy! That's what it's all about!
4. Me, me, me! That's what it's all about!
5. You, you, you! That's what it's all about!

Point to yourself during the fourth stanza, to others during the fifth stanza.

I'm with You

Terry K. Dittmer

Terry K. Dittmer

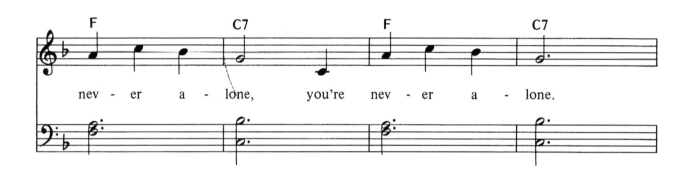
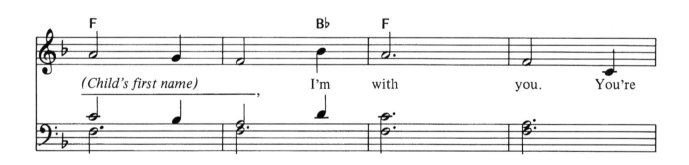
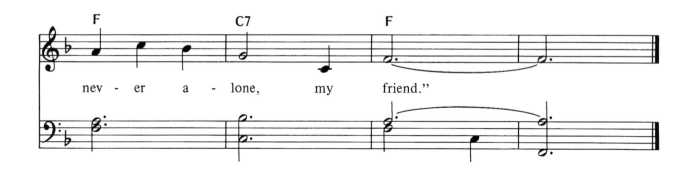

DAILY LIVING 33

Jesus Wants Me for a Helper

Dorothy N. Schultz   Dorothy N. Schultz

1. Je - sus wants me for a help - er When I work or when I play. I can show my love for Je - sus In the things I do or say.
2. I can tell some - one, "I love you," Be a friend and share my toys. I can show my love for Je - sus Help - ing oth - er girls and boys.
3. I can plant some pret - ty flow - ers, Wash the dish - es, pull the weeds. I can show my love for Je - sus Do - ing kind and lov - ing deeds.
4. I can help to set the ta - ble, Fold the clothes or make my bed. I can show my love for Je - sus Help - ing oth - ers as He said.

With younger children, teach one stanza at a time. After all stanzas are learned, see if they can recall the things they can do to help.

34 DAILY LIVING

Jesus, You Help

Nancy Carlson — Nancy Carlson

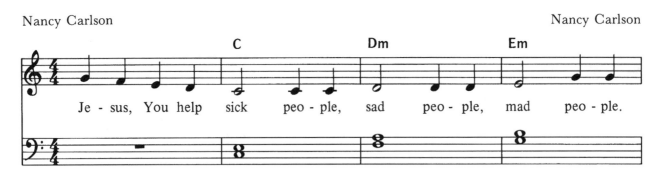
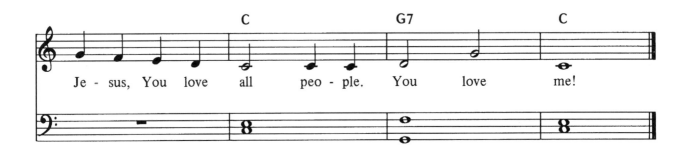

Je-sus, You help sick peo-ple, sad peo-ple, mad peo-ple.

Je-sus, You love all peo-ple. You love me!

Love in a Box

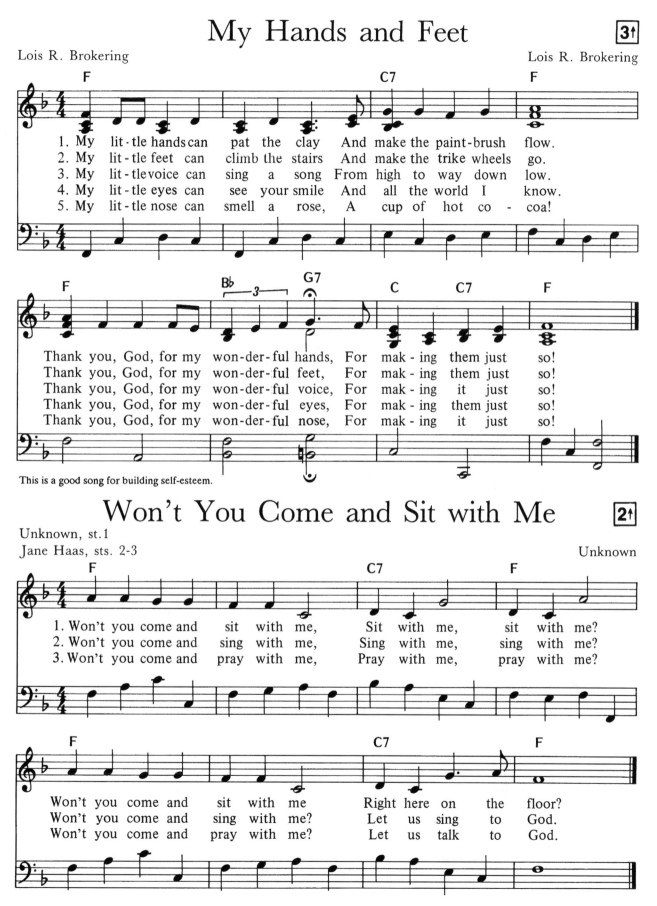

38 DAILY LIVING

When I'm Feeling Scared or Sad

Lois R. Brokering

Lois R. Brokering

Sing this song as a positive ending to one of those "bad days."

All Night, All Day

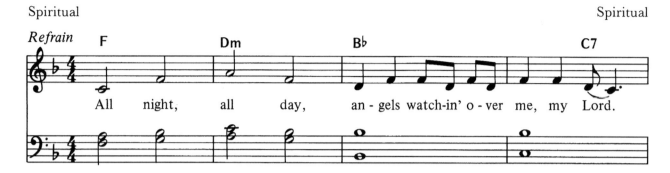

Closing Prayer

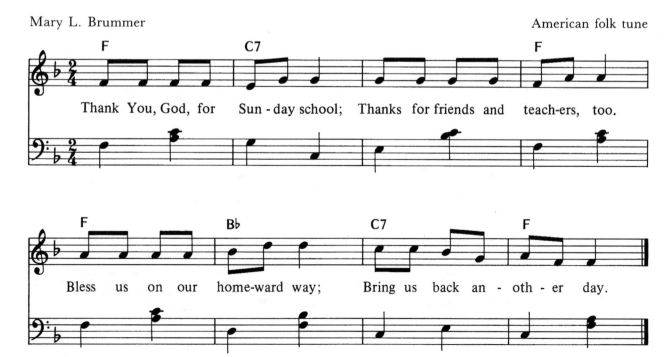

40 CLOSING

Good-bye

Lena S. Lawrence — Lena S. Lawrence

Good-bye, good-bye, To you and you and you.
Good-bye, good-bye, May God watch o-ver you.

Good-bye, Good-bye
(Hello, Hello)*

Elizabeth Sparrow — Elizabeth Sparrow

Good-bye, good-bye, good-bye, Good-bye, my friends, to you. God bless you ev-'ry-where you go, In all you say and do. Good-bye!

Hel-lo, hel-lo, hel-lo, Hel-lo, my friends, to you. God bless you ev-'ry-where you go, In all you say and do. Hel-lo!

* Opening song
Wave hands or shake hands on the last "good-bye" or "hello."

JESUS 41

Jesus Loves the Little Ones

Traditional

Traditional
Arr. by Edward Damerau, Jr.

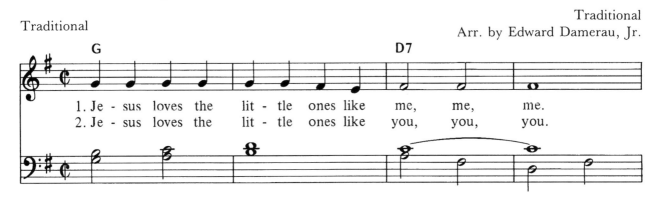
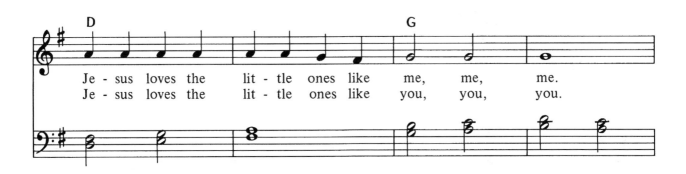
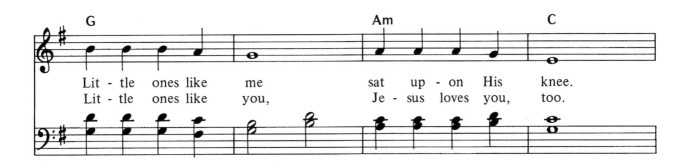
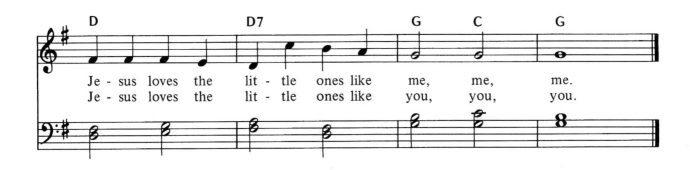

42 JESUS

Jesus Loves Me, This I Know

3↑

Anna B. Warner, 1820-1915   William B. Bradbury, 1816-68

1. Jesus loves me, this I know, For the Bible tells me so.
   Little ones to Him belong; They are weak, but He is strong.
2. Jesus loves me, He who died, Heaven's gate to open wide;
   He will wash away my sin, Let His little child come im.

Refrain
Yes, Jesus loves me, Yes, Jesus loves me,
Yes, Jesus loves me, The Bible tells me so.

Refrain

NAVAJO:
Jesus ayóó áshóní,
Jesus ayóó áshóní,
Jesus ayóó áshóní,
Bizaad yee shithl hal ne.

INDIAN:
Piyar karta, mujh ko,
Piyar karta, mujh ko,
Piyar karta, mujh ko,
Bibúl se m'allum hai.

SPANISH:
Sí, Cristo me ama;
Sí, Cristo me ama;
Sí, Cristo me ama;
La Biblia dice así.

CHINESE:
Ju Yesu nai wo,
Ju Yesu nai wo,
Ju Yesu nai wo,
Shung jing i ko ru wo.

AFRICAN:
Yesu antemwa,
Yesu antemwa,
Yesu antemwa,
Ilandwe lyanjeba.

See illustrations for signing this song on page 43.

JESUS 43

Jesus Is My Special Friend

4↑

Daniel Burow Carol Greene

1. Je - sus is my spe - cial Friend; He goes wher - e'er I go.
2. Je - sus is my spe - cial Friend, My Help - er kind and true,

When I'm bad, it makes Him sad, But still He loves me so.
Night and day, at work and play, And He is your Friend, too.

This song is especially good for skipping or dancing.

JESUS   LOVES   ME

44 JESUS

There Is a Name I Love to Hear

Frederick Whitfield, 1829-1904

American melody, 19th cent.

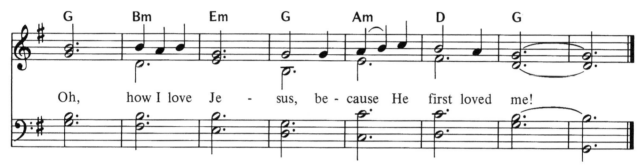

OH, HOW I LOVE JESUS

BECAUSE HE FIRST LOVED ME

JESUS 45

My Best Friend Is Jesus

Mildred Adair Stagg Mildred Adair Stagg

Children may think of additional responses in place of "Love Him" or "Thank Him."

MY BEST FRIEND IS JESUS

LOVE HIM THANK HIM

48 SCRIPTURE

Alleluia. Lord, to Whom Shall We Go

Lutheran Book of Worship, 1978

Richard Hillert
Arr. by Richard W. Gieseke

Children can learn this part of the liturgy sung in Lutheran services.

The B-I-B-L-E

Dwight Uphaus   Traditional

1. The B-I-B-L-E, It is God's Word to me; I will obey God's Holy Word, The B-I-B-L-E.
2. The B-I-B-L-E, Its *sto-ries help me see The love of Je-sus, God's own Son; The B-I-B-L-E.

* lessons

Text © 1980 by Lillenas Publishing Co. All rights reserved. Used by permission.

SCRIPTURE 49

The Best Book of All

Mary Royer
Charles Burkhart

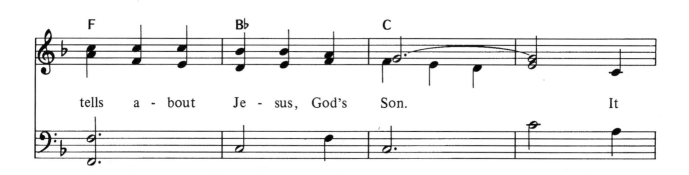

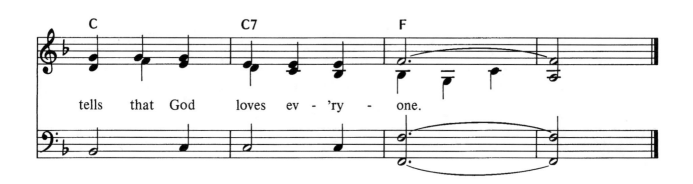

Psalm 8

52 SCRIPTURE

Rejoice in the Lord Always

Philippians 4:4

Anonymous

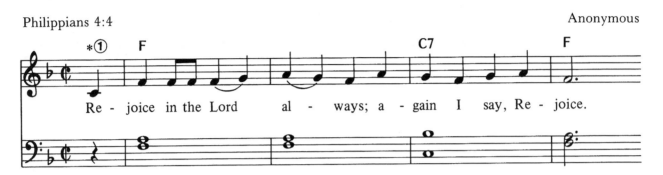

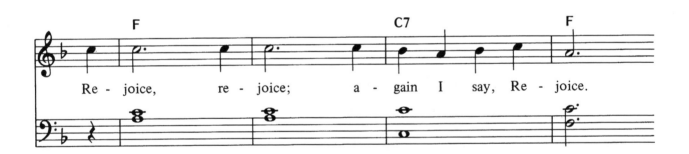
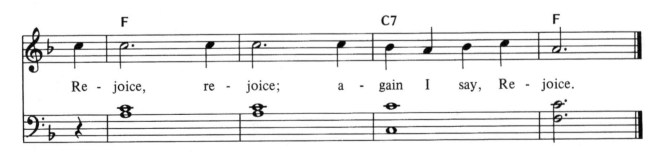

* May be sung as a round

Read the text from the Bible before singing this song. If necessary, explain the meaning of "rejoice."

54 SCRIPTURE

We Love

1 John 4:19

Ann F. Price

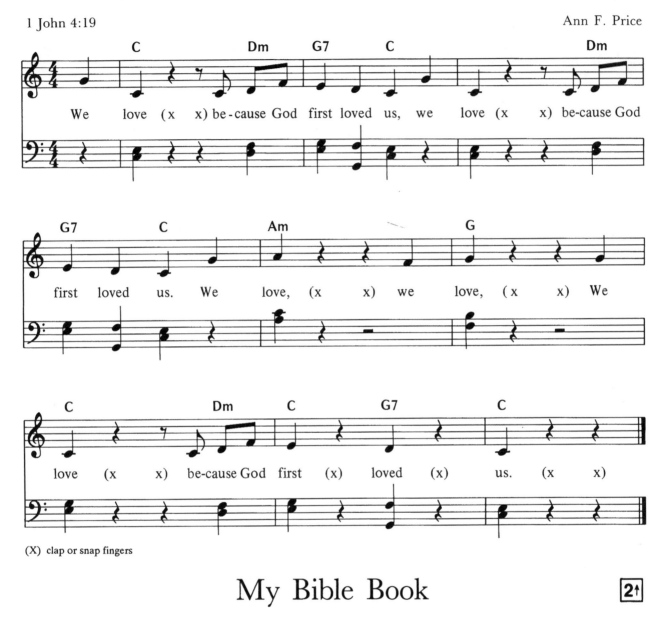

We love (x x) be-cause God first loved us, we love (x x) be-cause God first loved us. We love, (x x) we love, (x x) We love (x x) be-cause God first (x) loved (x) us. (x x)

(X) clap or snap fingers

My Bible Book

Johnnie B. Wood, alt.

Johnnie B. Wood

1. I o-pen my Bi-ble book and read, God loves me, God loves me.
2. I o-pen my Bi-ble book and read, God keeps me, God keeps me.
3. I o-pen my Bi-ble book and read, God helps me, God helps me.

Hold hands together as though they were two covers of a book. Open them to represent open pages as the song is sung; close the book after each stanza.

SCRIPTURE 55

Zacchaeus

Motions: (1) Hands in front, right palm raised above left palm.
(2) Move palms closer together.
(3) Alternate hands in climbing motion.
(4) Shade eyes with right hand and look down.
(5) Shade eyes with right hand and look up.
(6) Look up, gesture to Zacchaeus to come down.
(7) Clap hands on accented beat.

56 PRAISE AND THANKSGIVING

A Hymn of Glory Let Us Sing

The Venerable Bede, 673-735

Lasst uns erfreuen
Geistliche Kirchengesäng, Köln, 1623

This is the refrain for several well-known hymns. Children feel important when they can sing along in church.

Glory, Glory, Hallelujah

Spiritual   Spiritual

This song of praise introduces children to the spiritual.

PRAISE AND THANKSGIVING 57

Earth and All Stars

Herbert F. Brokering

Earth and All Stars
David N. Johnson, 1922-87

God Is So Good

Anonymous — Anonymous

1. God is so good, God is so good, God is so good, He's so good to me.
2. He cares for me, He cares for me, He cares for me, He's so good to me.
3. He loves me so, He loves me so, He loves me so, He's so good to me.
4. I praise His name, I praise His name, I praise His name, He's so good to me.

* Alternate key for guitar

58 PRAISE AND THANKSGIVING

Hallelujah! Praise Ye the Lord!

PRAISE AND THANKSGIVING 59

Happy All the Time

Try these actions: "inright" – point to self
"outright" – point away from self
"upright" – stand up
"downright" – sit down
"happy all the time" – clap hands

60 PRAISE AND THANKSGIVING

If You Feel Happy

Carol Greene Carol Greene

1. If you feel hap-py, If you feel hap-py, If you feel hap-py, Clap your hands with me. (Clap! Clap!)
2. If you feel sad, If you feel sad, If you feel sad, Cry a-long with me. (Boo-hoo!)
3. If you feel grump-y, If you feel grump-y, If you feel grump-y, Shout it out with me. (Oh, rats!)
4. If you feel fright-ened, If you feel fright-ened, If you feel fright-ened, Knock your knees with me. (Clop! Clop!)
5. If you feel lov-ing, If you feel lov-ing, If you feel lov-ing, Hug a friend with me. (Mmmm!)

* Alternate key for guitar

This song helps children accept various emotions.

62 PRAISE AND THANKSGIVING

I Have the Joy

Traditional / Traditional

PRAISE AND THANKSGIVING 63

Making Melody in My Heart

3↑

Unknown — Unknown

64 PRAISE AND THANKSGIVING

My God Is So Great

PRAISE AND THANKSGIVING

Praise God, from Whom All Blessings Flow

Thomas Ken, 1637-1711

Old Hundredth
Louis Bourgeois, c. 1510-c. 1561

Praise God, from whom all bless-ings flow; Praise Him, all crea-tures here be-low; Praise Him a-bove, O heav'n-ly host; Praise Fa-ther, Son, and Ho-ly Ghost.

Rise and Shine
(Arky, Arky)

Anonymous
Traditional

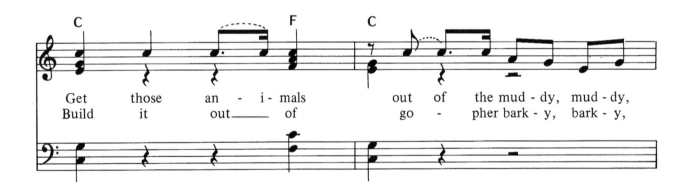

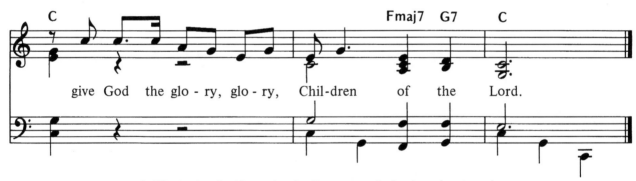

3. The animals, the animals, they came in by twosies, twosies,
   Animals, the animals, they came in by twosies, twosies,
   Elephants and kangaroosies, roosies,
   Children of the Lord.
   Refrain

4. It rained and poured for forty daysies, daysies,
   Rained and poured for forty daysies, daysies,
   Almost drove those animals crazies, crazies,
   Children of the Lord.
   Refrain

5. The sun came out, and dried up the landy, landy,
   Look! There's the sun, it dried up the landy, landy,
   Everything was fine and dandy, dandy,
   Children of the Lord.

   Refrain

68 PRAISE AND THANKSGIVING

Praise Him, Praise Him

3↑

Anonymous, c. 1890
Carey Bonner, 1859-1938

1. Praise Him, praise Him, all you little children; God is love, God is love. Praise Him, praise Him, all you little children; God is love, God is love.
2. Love Him, love Him, all you little children; God is love, God is love. Love Him, love Him, all you little children; God is love, God is love.
3. Thank Him, thank Him, all you little children; God is love, God is love. Thank Him, thank Him, all you little children; God is love, God is love.
4. Serve Him, serve Him, all you little children; God is love, God is love. Serve Him, serve Him, all you little children; God is love, God is love.

PRAISE HIM PRAISE HIM

PRAISE AND THANKSGIVING

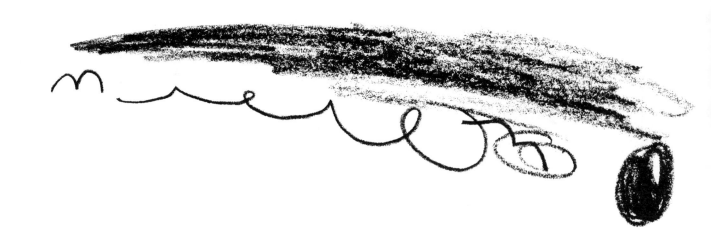

CREATION 73

Show pictures of each animal as you sing this song.

74 CREATION

Oh, Who Can Make a Flower

Grace W. Owens
Spanish tr. Ana Espada de Ortiz

Clara Lee Parker

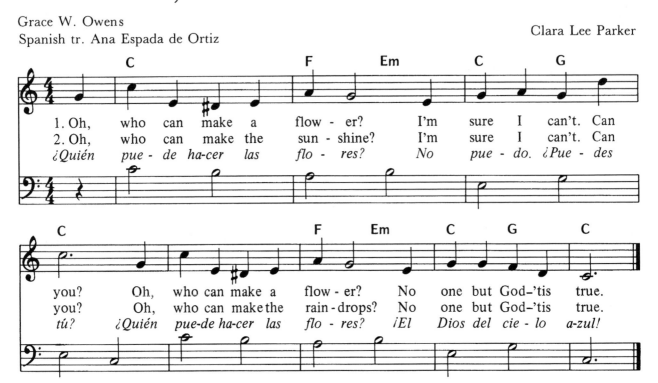

Give the children the opportunity to hear one of their favorite songs sung in Spanish.

Who Made the Sky So Bright and Blue

Jane Taylor, 1783-1824

Carol G. Glaeser, 1784-1829

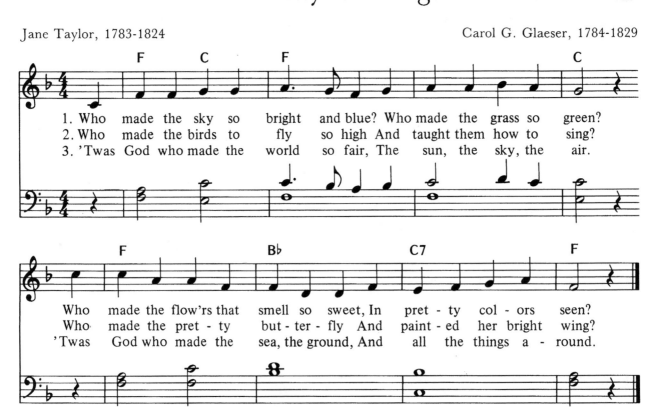

CREATION 75

God Made Me

Traditional   Traditional

1. God made me, God made me,
2. God loves me, God loves me,
3. God helps me, God helps me,
4. God keeps me, God keeps me,

In my Bi - ble book it says that God made me.
In my Bi - ble book it says that God loves me.
In my Bi - ble book it says that God helps me.
In my Bi - ble book it says that God keeps me.

God Gave Me Eyes

Margaret Crain McNeil   Margaret Crain McNeil

1. Blue, blue sky, Oh, I can see the sky.
2. Red, red rose, Oh, I can smell a rose.
3. Ding, dong, bell, Oh, I can hear a bell.
4. Yum, yum, yum, Oh, I can taste ice cream.
5. Mew, mew, mew, My kit - ty's fur is soft.

God gave me eyes So I can see the sky.
God gave a nose So I can smell a rose.
God gave me ears So I can hear a bell.
God gave a tongue So I can taste ice cream.
God gave me hands So I can feel how soft.

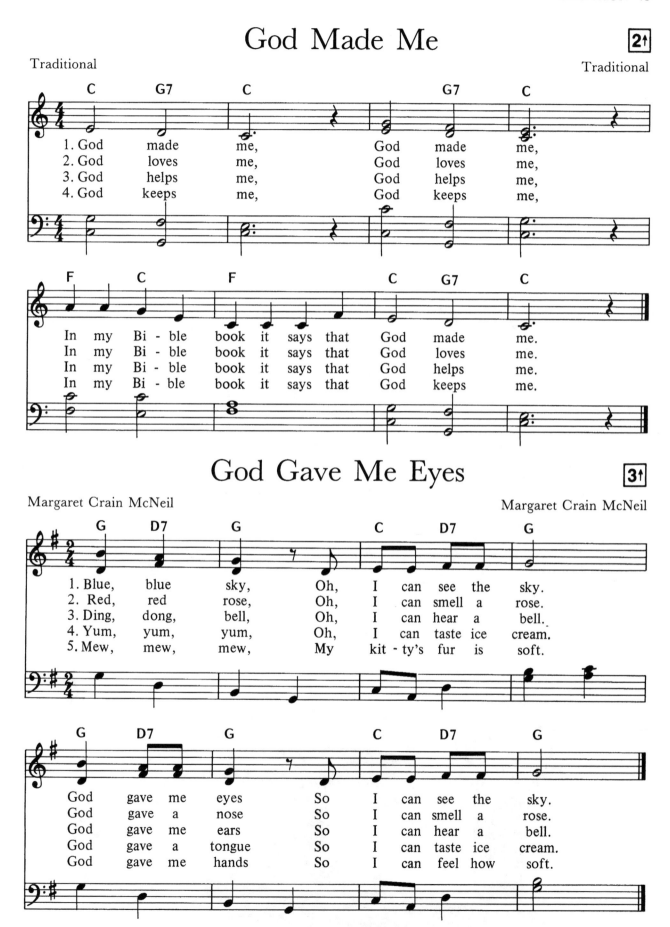

76 CREATION

God Made Me, Every Part You See

Daniel Burow
Unknown

God made me, Ev-'ry part you see: Ears and eyes and mouth and nos-es, Feet that with so man-y toes-es Skip and jump and hop, Al-most nev-er stop!

* Alternate key for guitar
Let the children point to the appropriate parts of their bodies. They might also skip, hop, or dance to the song.

ADVENT 79

Advent Wreath Song

Unknown   Unknown

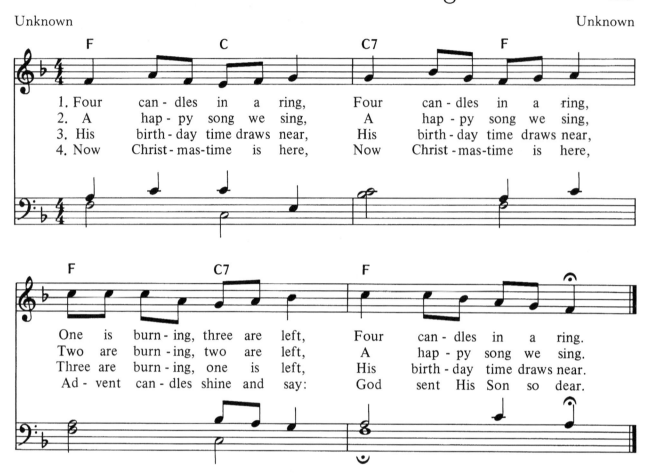

1. Four candles in a ring, Four candles in a ring, One is burning, three are left, Four candles in a ring.
2. A happy song we sing, A happy song we sing, Two are burning, two are left, A happy song we sing.
3. His birthday time draws near, His birthday time draws near, Three are burning, one is left, His birthday time draws near.
4. Now Christmas-time is here, Now Christmas-time is here, Advent candles shine and say: God sent His Son so dear.

This song may be sung as candles in an Advent wreath are lighted. Children may also form a moving wreath by walking in a circle. Four children stand in the center as the "candles." The teacher touches a child who is to be the "lighted candle." The child places hands on head for the "flame."

Away in a Manger
(Cradle Song)

Anonymous, c. 1883, sts. 1-2
John T. McFarland, 1851-1913, st. 3, alt.

Cradle Song
William J. Kirkpatrick, 1838-1921

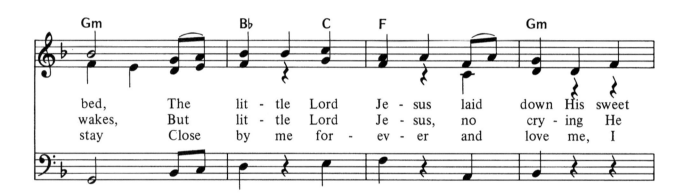

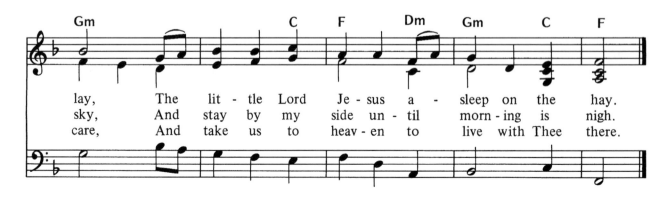

1. A-way in a man-ger, no crib for a bed, The lit-tle Lord Je-sus laid down His sweet head. The stars in the bright sky looked down where He lay, The lit-tle Lord Je-sus a-sleep on the hay.

2. The cat-tle are low-ing, the Ba-by a-wakes, But lit-tle Lord Je-sus, no cry-ing He makes. I love Thee, Lord Je-sus! Look down from the sky, And stay by my side un-til morn-ing is nigh.

3. Be near me, Lord Je-sus; I ask Thee to stay Close by me for-ev-er and love me, I pray. Bless all the dear chil-dren in Thy ten-der care, And take us to heav-en to live with Thee there.

CHRISTMAS 83

Away in a Manger

Author unknown, c. 1883, sts. 1-2
John T. McFarland, 1851-1913, st. 3, alt.

American, 19th cent.

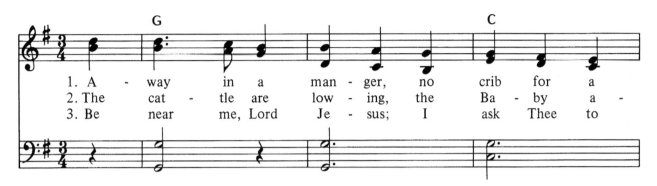

1. Away in a manger, no crib for a bed, The little Lord Jesus laid down His sweet head. The stars in the bright sky looked down where He lay, The little Lord Jesus asleep on the hay.
2. The cattle are lowing, the Baby awakes, But little Lord Jesus, no crying He makes. I love Thee, Lord Jesus! Look down from the sky, And stay by my side until morning is nigh.
3. Be near me, Lord Jesus; I ask Thee to stay Close by me forever and love me, I pray. Bless all the dear children in Thy tender care, And take us to heaven to live with Thee there.

84 CHRISTMAS

Go Tell It on the Mountain

Spiritual, Refrain
John W. Work II, 1871-1925, stanzas, alt.

Spiritual

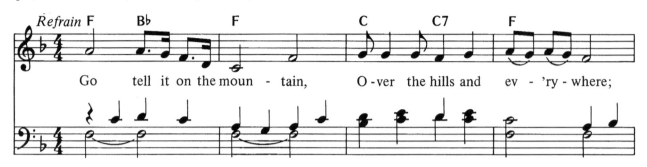

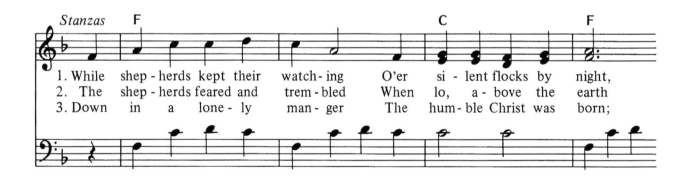

1. While shep-herds kept their watch-ing O'er si-lent flocks by night,
2. The shep-herds feared and trem-bled When lo, a-bove the earth
3. Down in a lone-ly man-ger The hum-ble Christ was born;

Be-hold, through-out the heav-ens There shone a ho-ly light.
Rang out the an-gel cho-rus That hailed our Sav-ior's birth.
And God sent us sal-va-tion That bless-ed Christ-mas morn.

For younger children, sing only the refrain.

CHRISTMAS 85

God Loves Me Dearly

August Rische, 19th cent.
Tr. composite, alt.

Gott ist die Liebe
German folk tune

1. God loves me dearly, Gives me salvation, God loves me dearly, Loves even me.
2. I was in bondage, Sin, death, and darkness; God's love was working To make me free.
3. He sent forth Jesus, That true Redeemer, He sent forth Jesus And set me free.
4. Jesus, my Savior, Himself did offer; Jesus, my Savior, Paid all I owed.
5. Now I will praise You, O dearest Savior; Now I will praise You All my life long.

Refrain
Therefore I'll say again: God loves me dearly, God loves me dearly, Loves even me.

CHRISTMAS 87

Oh, Come, All Ye Faithful

Attr. John F. Wade, c. 1711-86
Tr. composite

Adeste fideles
John F. Wade, c. 1711-86

Let Our Gladness Have No End

Bohemian carol, 15th cent.
Tr. unknown

Bohemian carol, 15th cent.

88 CHRISTMAS

Happy Birthday, Jesus

[4↑]

Barbara Kraft and Jane Haas

Jane Haas

1. On this happy Christmas Day, Praise to God our Father
For Your gift, our Savior dear. Happy birthday, Jesus!

2. Long ago you promised love — Love for ev-'ry sinner —
Love that came when Christ was born! Happy birthday, Jesus!

3. Angels came to tell the news To the lowly shepherds,
"Christ is born in Bethlehem!" Happy birthday, Jesus!

4. "Glory be to You, O Lord!" Sang the happy angels.
Shepherds ran to tell the Babe, "Happy birthday, Jesus!"

5. Wise men traveled many miles
Following a bright star
Till they found the Holy Child.
Happy birthday, Jesus!

6. We're so happy You were born,
Our best Friend and Savior.
Praise and thanks we sing to You.
Happy birthday, Jesus!

CHRISTMAS 89

Happy Birthday, Lord

Lynn Malmberg · Lynn Malmberg

90 CHRISTMAS

Mary Had a Baby

Spiritual, alt.   Spiritual

1. Mary had a baby, Yes, Lord! Mary had a baby, Yes, my Lord! Mary had a baby,
2. What did she name Him? Yes, Lord! What did she name Him? Yes, my Lord! What did she name Him?
3. She named the baby Jesus, Yes, Lord! She named the baby Jesus, Yes, my Lord! She named the baby Jesus,
4. Where was He born? Yes, Lord! Where was He born? Yes, my Lord! Where was He born?
5. Born in a manger, Yes, Lord! Born in a manger, Yes, my Lord! Born in a manger,

Yes, Lord! The little child of Bethlehem was born for us.

Christmas News

Carol Greene
Carol Greene

1. Hear us sing; News we bring: Jesus the Savior is born!
2. Hear the bell; Hear it tell: Jesus the Savior is born!
3. Hear the bird Spread the word: Jesus the Savior is born!

Hear us sing; News we bring: Jesus the Savior is born!
Hear the bell; Hear it tell: Jesus the Savior is born!
Hear the bird Spread the word: Jesus the Savior is born!

92 HOLY WEEK/EASTER

Jesus Came from Heaven

Dorothy N. Schultz

Sandown
James Frederick Swift, 1847-1931

1. Jesus came from heaven To the earth below, Lived and died to save me, For He loves me so.
2. Jesus rose on Easter; He's our Lord and King! To the risen Savior Alleluias sing!

Happy Day

Dorothy N. Schultz

Suo-Gân
Welsh folk song

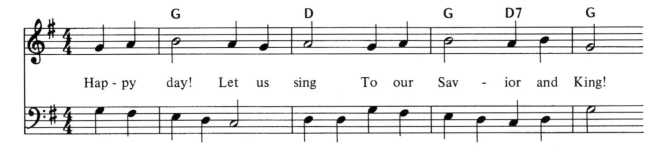

Happy day! Let us sing To our Savior and King!

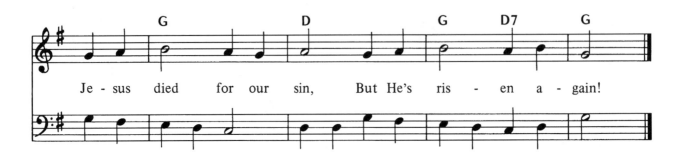

Jesus died for our sin, But He's risen again!

HOLY WEEK/EASTER 93

Glory Be to Jesus

Dorothy N. Schultz

Wem in Leidenstagen
Friedrich Filitz, 1804-76

1. Glo-ry be to Je-sus, Who, in per-fect love, Died to be my Sav-ior, Sent from heav'n a-bove.
2. Glo-ry be to Je-sus, Ris-en Lord and King; On this hap-py Eas-ter Al-le-lu-ias sing!

The new words to this familiar hymn make it more understandable for young children.

Do You Know Who Died for Me

O. William Luecke, 1953

O. William Luecke, 1953

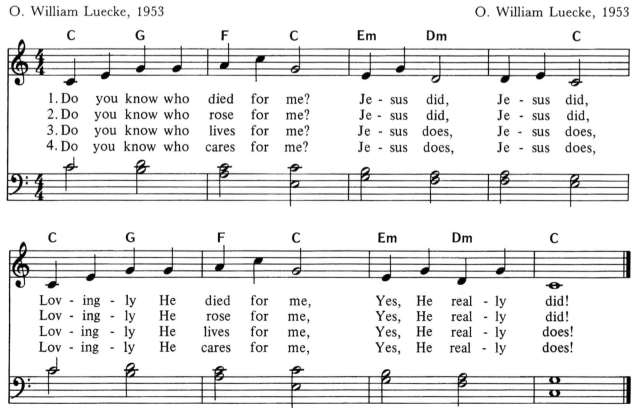

1. Do you know who died for me? Je-sus did, Je-sus did, Lov-ing-ly He died for me, Yes, He real-ly did!
2. Do you know who rose for me? Je-sus did, Je-sus did, Lov-ing-ly He rose for me, Yes, He real-ly did!
3. Do you know who lives for me? Je-sus does, Je-sus does, Lov-ing-ly He lives for me, Yes, He real-ly does!
4. Do you know who cares for me? Je-sus does, Je-sus does, Lov-ing-ly He cares for me, Yes, He real-ly does!

94 HOLY WEEK/EASTER

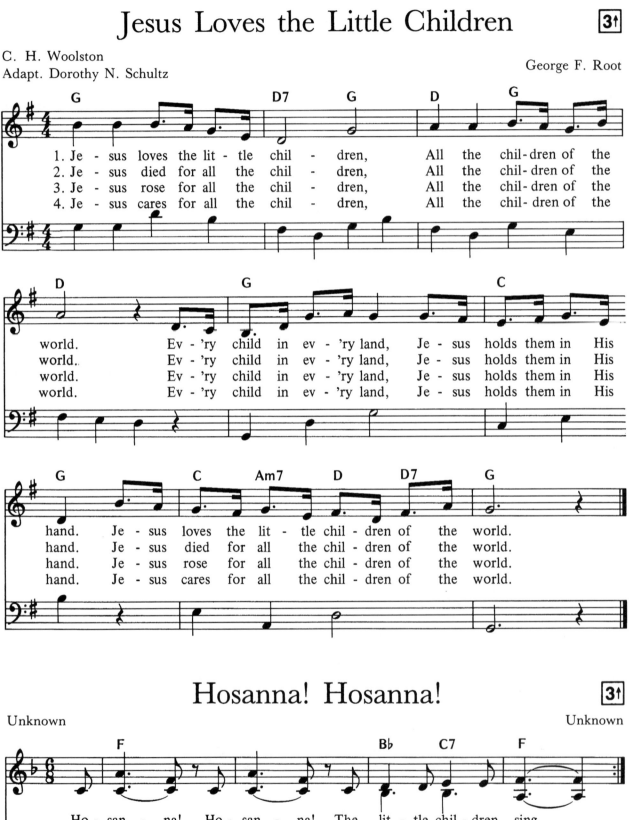

HOLY WEEK/EASTER 95

This Is the Feast

John W. Arthur, 1922-80

Richard Hillert

Children can learn this part of the liturgy sung in Lutheran services.

Christ the Lord Is Risen Today; Alleluia

Latin sequence, c. 1100
Tr. Jane E. Leeson, 1809-81

Llanfair
Robert Williams, c. 1781-1821

This is the first line of the familiar Easter hymn.

96 HOLY WEEK/EASTER

Jesus Christ Is Risen Today

Latin carol, 14th cent.
Tr. *Lyra Davidica,* London, 1708

Easter Hymn
Lyra Davidica, London, 1708

This is the first line of the familiar Easter hymn.

Christ the Lord Is Risen Today

Charles Wesley, 1707-88

Orientis partibus
French, 13th cent.

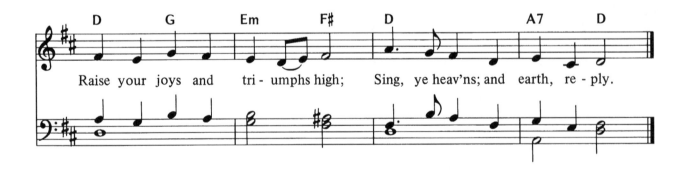

BAPTISM 97

I Was Baptized

Arnold C. Mueller, 1891-1980, alt.

Orientis partibus
French, 13th cent.

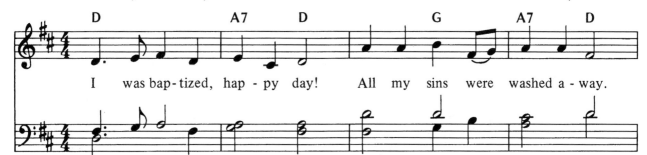

I was bap-tized, hap-py day! All my sins were washed a-way.
God looked down on me and smiled. I be-came His own dear child.

Baptism Song

Dorothy N. Schultz

Dorothy N. Schultz

God is my heav'n-ly Fa-ther, I know that He loves me. The day when I was bap-tized, I joined His fam-i-ly.

98 BAPTISM

Child of God

Anonymous, st. 1
Jaroslav J. Vajda, sts. 2-5

Southern folk song

1. If anybody asks you who I am, who I am, who I am, If anybody asks you who I am, Say that I'm a child of God.
2. If anybody asks you how I am, how I am, how I am, If anybody asks you how I am, Say that I'm alive and free.
3. If anybody asks you what that means, what that means, what that means, If anybody asks you what that means, Say that I was born again.
4. If anybody asks you where I'm going, where I'm going, where I'm going, If anybody asks you where I'm going, Say that I am going to heav'n.
5. If anybody asks you who's my Friend, who's my Friend, who's my Friend, If anybody asks you who's my Friend, Say that Jesus is His name.

* Alternate key for guitar

WITNESS 99

Come and Go with Me

Anonymous   Traditional

1. Come and go with me to my Father's house,
2. Ev-'ry-thing's all right in my Father's house,
3. Jesus is the Way to my Father's house,
4. There is room for all in my Father's house,

To my Father's house, To my Father's house; Come and go with me
In my Father's house, In my Father's house; Ev-'ry-thing's all right
To my Father's house, To my Father's house; Jesus is the Way
In my Father's house, In my Father's house; There is room for all

to my Father's house, Where there's joy, joy, joy!
in my Father's house, Where there's joy, joy, joy!
to my Father's house, Where there's joy, joy, joy!
in my Father's house, Where there's joy, joy, joy!

Use this for a moving song as the children move from the classroom to the church.

I Can Tell

Gretchen Anderson   Gretchen Anderson

1. I can tell, I can tell. Listen closely. I can tell.
2. Jesus loves You and me. Can you hear me? I can tell.
3. We are His, Ev'ry one. Hear me say it. I can tell.
4. Jesus died, Rose again. What good news! Oh, I can tell.

100 WITNESS

God Loves You

Unknown / Unknown

God loves you, and I love you, And that's the way it's gon-na be!
God loves you, and I love you, And that's the way it's gon-na be!

I Love to Tell the Story

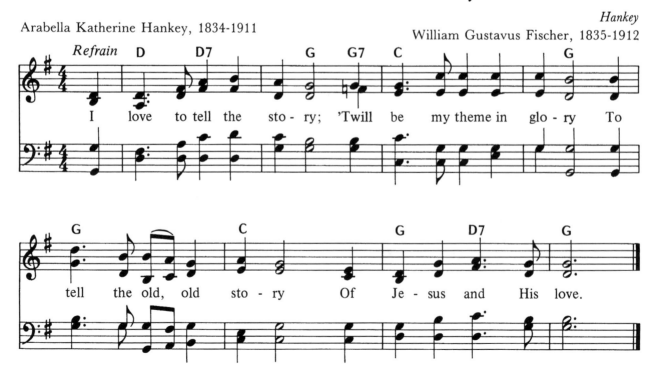

Arabella Katherine Hankey, 1834-1911 / *Hankey* / William Gustavus Fischer, 1835-1912

Refrain: I love to tell the sto-ry; 'Twill be my theme in glo-ry To tell the old, old sto-ry Of Je-sus and His love.

WITNESS 101

He's Got the Whole World in His Hands

Spiritual   Spiritual

1. He's got the whole world in His hands, He's got the whole wide world in His hands, He's got the whole world in His hands, He's got the whole world in His hands.
2. He's got the wind and the rain in His hands, He's got the sun and the moon in His hands, He's got the wind and the rain in His hands, He's got the whole world in His hands.
3. He's got the tiny little baby in His hands, He's got the tiny little baby in His hands, He's got the tiny little baby in His hands, He's got the whole world in His hands.
4. He's got you and me, brother, in His hands, He's got you and me, sister, in His hands, He's got you and me, brother, in His hands, He's got the whole world in His hands.

Children may suggest additional stanzas by naming things God created.

102 WITNESS

God Made You

David Morstad   David Morstad

Address the first part of the song to an individual, and the second part ("Open your eyes") to the group.

Go Tell

Lois R. Brokering Lois R. Brokering

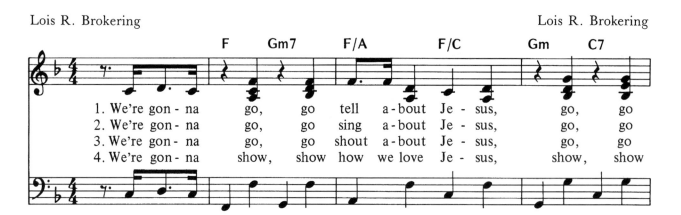

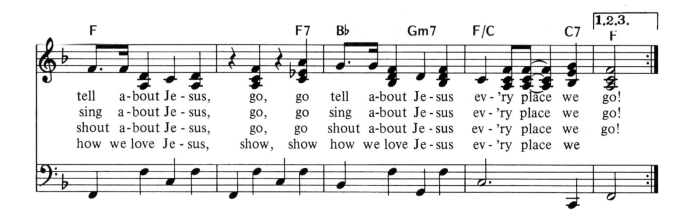

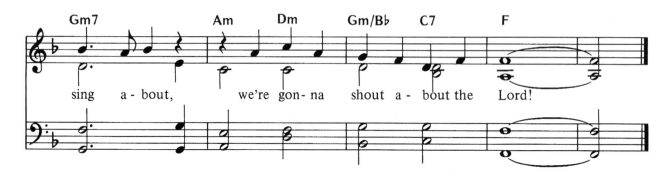

106 WITNESS

We Are the Church

Richard Avery and Donald Marsh
Richard Avery and Donald Marsh

I am the church! You are the church! We are the church together! All who follow Jesus All around the world! Yes, we're the church together!

Copyright © 1972 by Hope Publishing Company, Carol Stream, IL 60188. All Rights Reserved. Used by Permission.

Piggyback Songs

ADVENT SONG [2↑]

(Tune: "Jimmy Crack Corn")

Light one candle, Advent's here. (*Hold up one finger.*)
Light one candle, Advent's here.
Light one candle, Advent's here.
Christmas time is near. (*Clap two times.*)

(*Additional stanzas: two candles, three candles, four candles.*)

AUTUMN, AUTUMN, COMING FAST [4↑]

(Tune: "Twinkle, Twinkle, Little Star")

Autumn, autumn, coming fast,
Falling leaves and drying grass.
Apples, leaves, and nuts are falling.
Mr. Wind so cold is calling.
Autumn, autumn everywhere,
Jesus lets me know He cares.

CHRISTMAS IS A TIME OF JOYS [3↑]

(Tune: "Jesus Loves Me")

Christmas is a time of joys
For all people, girls and boys.
Joyfully today we sing,
Jesus is our newborn King.
Yes, I love Jesus!
Yes, I love Jesus!
Yes, I love Jesus!
He is our newborn King.

FRIENDS [3↑]

(Tune: "Mary Had a Little Lamb")

1. Will you be a friend of mine,
   Friend of mine, friend of mine?
   Will you be a friend of mine
   And dance around with me?

2. My best Friend is Jesus Christ,
   Jesus Christ, Jesus Christ.
   My best Friend is Jesus Christ.
   And He is your Friend, too.

GO TELL YOUR BROTHER [3↑]

(Tune: "Go Tell Aunt Rhody")

Go tell your brother,
Go tell your sister,
Go tell your mother,
That Jesus died for them.
Go tell your brother,
Go tell your sister,
Go tell your mother,
That Jesus died for them.
Go tell the people,
Go tell the people,
Go tell the people
That Christ loves you and me.

GOD CHOSE ME [4↑]

(Tune: "Twinkle, Twinkle, Little Star")

God chose me and God chose you.
We have special work to do!
Helping people every day,
We can sing and we can pray.
God chose me and God chose you;
We have special work to do.

GOD IS NEAR ME [4↑]

(Tune: "Are You Sleeping?")

God is near me, God is near me,
All the time, all the time.
When the lightning clashes,
When the thunder crashes,
God's in charge, God's in charge.

HELPERS, HELPERS, EVERYWHERE [4↑]

(Tune: "Twinkle, Twinkle, Little Star")

Helpers, helpers, everywhere,
Helping us with loving care.
God sends helpers big and small.
God sends helpers to us all.
Helpers, helpers, everywhere,
Helping us with loving care.

I AM SPECIAL [2↑]

(*Tune: "Are You Sleeping?"*)

I am special, I am special.
God sent me, God sent me.
To my mom and daddy, to my mom and daddy.
They love me, they love me.

IT'S A NEW DAY [3↑]

(*Tune: "Are You Sleeping?"*)

It's a new day, it's a new day
Given by God, given by God.
Join the celebration, join the celebration!
Sing His praise! Sing His praise!

JESUS IS OUR FRIEND [2↑]

(*Tune: "The Farmer in the Dell"*)

1. Jesus is our friend,
   Jesus is our friend.
   Pray, praise, and sing hooray!
   Jesus is our friend.

2. Jesus loves us so,
   Jesus loves us so.
   Pray, praise, and sing hooray!
   Jesus loves us so!

JESUS LOVES CHILDREN [4↑]

(*Tune: "Rock-a-bye Baby"*)

1. Jesus loves children, Jesus loves me,
   Jesus loves you with love tenderly.
   Jesus loves all, no matter how small,
   That's why I love Jesus better than all.

2. When I am playing, Jesus takes care,
   When I am sleeping, Jesus is there.
   And when I die, my Jesus will come,
   And safe in His arms He'll carry me home.

3. Tell all your playmates Jesus loves them,
   Tell them the story, tell it again.
   Bring them to Jesus, where they will hear
   That Jesus loves children, precious and dear.

RING THE BELLS [2↑]

(*Tune: "Are You Sleeping?"*)

Ring the bells, ring the bells.
Christmas bells, Christmas bells.
It is Jesus' birthday, it is Jesus' birthday.
Can you tell? Can you tell?

THE HATS ARE IN THE DRUM [3↑]

(*Tune: "The Farmer in the Dell"*)

The hats are in the drum,
The hats are in the drum.
Take one out and put it on
And see what you become.

(*After a child takes out a hat and puts it on, sing the second stanza:*)

I am (*a fire fighter*),
I am (*a fire fighter*).

God gives us helpers everywhere.
I am (*a fire fighter*).

(*Repeat song for other occupations – a crossing guard, a bus driver, a baker, a waitress, an officer, a mail carrier, a store clerk, etc.*)

THIS IS THE WAY WE DRESS FOR CHURCH [3↑]

(*Tune: "Here We Go Round the Mulberry Bush"*)

1. This is the way we dress for church,
   (*Stretch arms above head as if putting on a sweater*)
   Dress for church, dress for church;
   This is the way we dress for church,
   Every Sunday morning.

2. This is the way we walk to church,
   (*Walk happily in place*)
   Walk to church, walk to church;
   This is the way we walk to church,
   Every Sunday morning.

3. This is the way we climb the steps,
   (*Climb imaginary steps*)
   Climb the steps, climb the steps;
   This is the way we climb the steps,
   Every Sunday morning.

4. This is the way we sit in church,
   (Sit up straight and attentive)
   Sit in church, sit in church;
   This is the way we sit in church,
   Every Sunday morning.

5. This is the way we stand and sing,
   *(Stand and pretend to hold a hymnal
   in front of you.)*
   Stand and sing, stand and sing;
   This is the way we stand and sing,
   Every Sunday morning.

6. This is the way we pray in church,
   (Bow head and fold hands)
   Pray in church, pray in church;
   This is the way we pray in church,
   Every Sunday morning.

7. This is the way we leave the church,
   (Walk happily in place)
   Leave the church, leave the church;
   This is the way we leave the church,
   Every Sunday morning.

WE WILL HELP THE LITTLE CHILDREN [4↑]

(Tune: "Jesus Loves the Little Children")

We will help the little children,
Little children of the world.
We will give our gifts of love,
Show our love to God above.
We will help the little children of the world.

WHERE IS JESUS? [3↑]

(Tune: "Are You Sleeping?")

Where is Jesus? Where is Jesus?
Here He is! Here He is!
With me on the playground, with me on the
   playground.
Yes, He is, yes, He is.

(Help the children think of other answers to sing in place of "With me on the playground." Sing your new stanzas together.)

WHERE IS JESUS? EVERYWHERE [3↑]

(Tune: "Are You Sleeping?")

Where is Jesus? Where is Jesus?
Everywhere, everywhere.
What is Jesus doing? What is Jesus doing?
Taking care, taking care.

WILL YOU PRAY FOR ME TODAY? [3↑]

(Tune: "Mary Had a Little Lamb")

1. Will you pray for me today,
   Me today, me today?
   Will you pray for me today,
   And show me Jesus' love?

2. Yes, I'll pray for you today,
   You today, you today,
   Yes, I'll pray for you today,
   And show you Jesus' love!

Acknowledgments

Every effort has been made to determine the ownership of all texts, tunes and harmonizations used in this edition and to secure permission for their use. Any oversight that may have occurred will be duly corrected and properly acknowledged in future editions if brought to the publisher's attention.

The following copyright items are acknowledged:

A Hymn of Glory Let Us Sing
   Setting: By Ralph Vaughan Williams, 1872-1958. From the *English Hymnal;* simplified and reprinted by permission of Oxford University Press.

Advent Song
   Text: From *Integrating the Faith*, Vol. 1, Teachers Guide. Copyright ©1986 Concordia Publishing House.

Advent Wreath Song
   Text and tune: Copyright © Augsburg Publishing House. Reprinted by permission.

All Night, All Day
   Setting: Copyright © 1989 Concordia Publishing House.

Alleluia. Lord, to Whom Shall We Go
   Text and tune: Copyright © 1978 *Lutheran Book of Worship*. By permission of Concordia Publishing House.
   Setting: From *Songs of God's Love*. Copyright © 1984 Concordia Publishing House.

Amigos de Cristo
   Text, tune, and setting: © 1983, John C. Ylvisaker. Used by permission, Lyons Management Systems, 4308 Mackey Ave. So., Minneapolis, MN 55424.

As Each Happy Christmas
   Setting: From *A Child's Garden of Song*. Copyright © 1949 Concordia Publishing House.

Autumn, Autumn, Coming Fast
   Text: From *Integrating the Faith*, Vol. 1, Teachers Guide. Copyright © 1986 Concordia Publishing House.

Away in a Manger (*Cradle Song*)
   Setting: Ralph Vaughan Williams, 1872-1958. From *Enlarged Songs of Praise* 1931; reprinted by permission of Oxford University Press.

Baptism Song
   Text, tune, and setting: Copyright © 1989 Concordia Publishing House.

Chatter with the Angels
   Text: From the book, MUSICAL GAMES, FINGERPLAYS AND RHYTHMIC ACTIVITIES FOR EARLY CHILDHOOD by Marian Wirth, Verna Stassevitch, Rita Shotwell, Patricia Stemmler, © 1983. Published by Parker Publishing Company, Inc., West Nyack, New York.

Child of God
   Text and setting: Sts. 2–5 and setting from *Songs of God's Love*. Copyright © 1984 Concordia Publishing House.

Christ the Lord Is Risen Today
   Setting: From *A Child's Garden of Song*. Copyright © 1949 Concordia Publishing House.

Christmas Is a Time of Joys
   Text: From *Integrating the Faith*, Vol. 1, Teachers Guide. Copyright © 1986 Concordia Publishing House.

Christmas News
   Text, tune, and setting: From *The Little Christian's Songbook*. Copyright © 1975 Concordia Publishing House.

Closing Prayer
   Text: Copyright © 1974 Concordia Publishing House.

Come and Go with Me
   Setting: J. K. Hiller. From *My God–My Faith–My Life*, 1972 VBS. Copyright © 1972 Concordia Publishing House.

Dear Father in Heaven
   Setting: From *Little Children, Sing to God!* Copyright © 1960 Concordia Publishing House.

Do You Know Who Died for Me
   Text and tune: Copyright 1953 O. Wm. Luecke. Used by permission.
   Setting: From *Songs of God's Love*. Copyright © 1984 Concordia Publishing House.

Earth and All Stars
   Text, tune, and setting: Copyright © Augsburg Publishing House. Reprinted by permission.

Father, Bless the Gifts We Bring You
   Setting: From *Songs of God's Love*. Copyright © 1984 Concordia Publishing House.

Father, I Adore You
   Text and tune: By Terrye Coelho © 1972 Maranatha! Music. All rights reserved. International copyright secured. Used by permission.

Friends
   Text: From *Integrating the Faith*, Vol. 1, Teachers Guide. Copyright © 1986 Concordia Publishing House.

Gathering Song
   Text, tune, and setting: Copyright © 1989 Concordia Publishing House.

Glory Be to Jesus
   Text and setting: Text copyright © 1989 Concordia Publishing House. Setting from *Songs of God's Love*. Copyright © 1984 Concordia Publishing House.

Go Tell
   Text, tune, and setting: © 1986 Herb Associates, 11641 Palmer Rd., Bloomington, MN 55437. Used by permission.

Go Tell It on the Mountain
   Text: Stanzas by permission of Mrs. John W. Work III.
   Setting: From *Songs of God's Love*. Copyright © 1984 Concordia Publishing House.

Go Tell Your Brother
   Text: From *Integrating the Faith*, Vol. 1, Teachers Guide. Copyright © 1986 Concordia Publishing House.

God Chose Me
   Text: From *Jesus Loves Me*, Teachers Guide. Copyright © 1975 Concordia Publishing House.

God Gave Me Eyes
   Text, tune, and setting: By Margaret Crain McNeil, from NURSERY SONGS AND RHYTHMS, © Copyright 1953 by Judson Press. Used by permission.

God Has Sent His Angels Down
   Text and setting: Text from *Jesus My Savior*. Copyright © 1984 Concordia Publishing House. Setting from *A Child's Garden of Song*. Copyright © 1949 Concordia Publishing House.

God Is Near
   Text and setting: From *A Child's Garden of Song*. Copyright © 1949 Concordia Publishing House.

God Is Near Me
   Text: From *Jesus My Friend*, Teachers Guide. Copyright © 1985 Concordia Publishing House.

God Is So Good
   Setting: From *Songs of God's Love*. Copyright © 1984 Concordia Publishing House.

God Loves Me Dearly
   Setting: From *A Child's Garden of Song*. Copyright © 1949 Concordia Publishing House.

God Loves You
   Setting: Copyright © 1989 Concordia Publishing House.

God Made Me
   Setting: Copyright © 1989 Concordia Publishing House.

God Made Me, Every Part You See
   Text and setting: From *The Little Christian's Songbook*. Copyright © 1975 Concordia Publishing House.

God Made You
   Text, tune, and setting: © 1981 by David Morstad, Watertown, WI. Used by permission.

God, Our Father, Hear Your Children
   Setting: From *Joyfully Sing*. Copyright © 1961 Concordia Publishing House.

God's a Father Kind and True
   Text, tune, and setting: From *A Child's Garden of Song*. Copyright © 1949 Concordia Publishing House.

God's Care
   Text and tune: © 1948, Scripture Press Foundation. All rights reserved. © 1976, renewed by Scripture Press Publications, Inc. All rights reserved. Used by permission.

Good-bye
   Text, tune, and setting: Reprinted from LITTLE ONES SING. Copyright 1962 by Gospel Light Publications, Ventura, CA 93003. Used by permission.

Good-bye, Good-bye
   Text, tune, and setting: From *The Little Christian's Songbook*. Copyright © 1975 Concordia Publishing House.

Happy All the Time
   Tune: Copyright © 1944 and renewed 1972 by Singspiration Music/ASCAP. All rights reserved. Used by permission of The Benson Company, Inc., Nashville, Tennessee.

Happy Birthday, Jesus
   Text, tune, and setting: Text and tune from *Interaction*. Copyright © 1986 Concordia Publishing House. Setting copyright © 1989 Concordia Publishing House.

Happy Birthday, Lord
   Text and tune: Copyright © 1987 by Lynn M. Malmberg. Used by permission.
   Setting: Copyright © 1989 Concordia Publishing House.

Happy Birthday to You
   Text: St. 1 © 1935 SUMMY-BIRCHARD MUSIC (renewed). All rights reserved. Used by permission.

Happy Day
   Text and setting: Copyright © 1989 Concordia Publishing House.

Happy Now We Gather
   Text: Copyright © 1974 Concordia Publishing House.

Hello, Hello
   Text, tune, and setting: From *The Little Christian's Songbook*. Copyright © 1975 Concordia Publishing House.

Hello, Hello! How Are You?
   Text, tune, and setting: Reprinted by permission from YOUNG CHILDREN SING copyright © 1967 Augsburg Publishing House.

Helpers, Helpers, Everywhere
   Text: From *Jesus My Friend*, Teachers Guide. Copyright © 1985 Concordia Publishing House.

He's Got the Whole World in His Hands
   Setting: From *Joyful Sounds*. Copyright © 1977 Concordia Publishing House.

Hosanna! Hosanna!
   Text, tune, and setting: Reprinted by permission from LET'S SING, copyright © Augsburg Publishing House.

I Am Sorry, Jesus
   Text and setting: Copyright © 1989 Concordia Publishing House.

I Am Special
   Text: From *Jesus Loves Me*, Teachers Guide. Copyright © 1985 Concordia Publishing House.

I Am Trusting You, Lord Jesus
   Text and setting: Text copyright © 1989 Concordia Publishing House. Setting from *A Child's Garden of Song*. Copyright © 1949 Concordia Publishing House.

I Can Stamp
   Text, tune, and setting: From *The Little Christian's Songbook*. Copyright © 1975 Concordia Publishing House.

I Can Tell
   Text, tune, and setting: From *The Little Christian's Songbook*. Copyright © 1975 Concordia Publishing House.

I Have a Hello in My Heart
   Text and tune: © Copyright, 1978, World Library Publications, Inc. All rights reserved. Used with permission.

I Have Hands
   Text, tune, and setting: From LITTLE ONES SING, Praise Book Publications. Copyright © 1962 G/L Publications. Used by permission.

I Like to Be in Sunday School
   Text: Copyright © Concordia Publishing House.

I Was Baptized
   Text and setting: From *A Child's Garden of Song*. Copyright © 1949 Concordia Publishing House.

If You Feel Happy
   Text, tune, and setting: From *The Little Christian's Songbook*. Copyright © 1975 Concordia Publishing House.

I'm as Happy as Can Be
   Text and tune: Copyright © O. Wm. Luecke. Used by permission.

I'm Glad
   Text and setting: From *The Little Christian's Songbook*. Copyright © 1975 Concordia Publishing House.

I'm Growing
   Text, tune, and setting: © 1988 Herb Associates, 11641 Palmer Rd., Bloomington, MN 55437. Used by permission.

I'm Sorry!
   Text, tune, and setting: © 1988 Herb Associates, 11641 Palmer Rd., Bloomington, MN 55437. Used by permission.

I'm with You
   Text, tune, and setting: Copyright © 1989 Concordia Publishing House.

In a Little Stable
   Text, tune, and setting: From *Little Children, Sing to God!* Copyright © 1960 Concordia Publishing House.

It's Good to Give Thanks
 Setting: © 1980 Lillenas Publishing Company. All Rights Reserved. Used by permission.

Jesus Came from Heaven
 Text and setting: Text copyright © 1989 Concordia Publishing House. Setting from *A Child's Garden of Song*. Copyright © 1949 Concordia Publishing House.

Jesus Christ Is Risen Today
 Setting: From *Joyful Sounds*. Copyright © 1977 Concordia Publishing House.

Jesus Is My Special Friend
 Text, tune, and setting: From *The Little Christian's Songbook*. Copyright © 1975 Concordia Publishing House.

Jesus Is Our Friend
 Text: From *Integrating the Faith,* Vol. 1, Teachers Guide. Copyright © 1986 Concordia Publishing House.

Jesus Listens When I Pray
 Tune: From *Little Children, Sing to God!* Copyright © 1960 Concordia Publishing House.

Jesus Loves Children
 Text: By H. W. Gockel. From *Little Children, Sing to God!* Copyright © 1960 Concordia Publishing House.

Jesus Loves Me, This I Know
 Setting: From *A Child's Garden of Song*. Copyright © 1949 Concordia Publishing House.

Jesus Loves the Little Children
 Text and setting: Copyright © 1989 Concordia Publishing House.

Jesus Loves the Little Ones
 Setting: Reprinted from *Living Faith Series*, Parent/Age 2, Term II, Copyright © 1987 Parish Life Press. Used by permission of Augsburg Fortress.

Jesus, Our Good Friend
 Text, tune, and setting: From *The Little Christian's Songbook*. Copyright © 1975 Concordia Publishing House.

Jesus Wants Me for a Helper
 Text, tune, and setting: Copyright © 1989 Concordia Publishing House.

Jesus! What a Name
 Text, tune, and setting: © 1981 Herbert Brokering, 11641 Palmer Rd., Bloomington, MN 55437. Used by permission.

Jesus, You Help
 Text, tune, and setting: Copyright © 1989 Concordia Publishing House.

Let Our Gladness Have No End
 Setting: Copyright © 1978 *Lutheran Book of Worship*. By permission of Concordia Publishing House.

Let Us Sing for Joy!
 Text and setting: Text from *Our Life in Christ*, Quarter 3, Kindergarten Lesson Leaflets. Copyright © 1989 Concordia Publishing House. Setting by J. K. Hiller. From *My God–My Faith–My Life,* 1972 VBS. Copyright © 1972 Concordia Publishing House.

Light One Candle
 Text, tune, and setting: © 1976 by Hinshaw Music. Reprinted by permission 1-27-89.

Love in a Box
 Text, tune, and setting: Copyright © Concordia Publishing House.

Love, Love, Love
 Text, tune, and setting: Copyright © Augsburg Publishing House. Reprinted by permission.

Making Melody in My Heart
 Setting: Copyright © 1989 Concordia Publishing House.

Mary Had a Baby
 Setting: Copyright © 1989 Concordia Publishing House.

My Best Friend Is Jesus
 Text, tune, and setting: © Copyright 1939. Renewal 1967 Broadman Press. All rights reserved. Used by permission.

My God Is So Great
 Setting: Copyright © 1989 Concordia Publishing House.

My Hands and Feet
 Text, tune, and setting: © 1988 Herb Associates, 11641 Palmer Rd., Bloomington, MN 55437. Used by permission.

Oh, Who Can Make a Flower
 Text: Spanish stanza from *Culto Cristiano*. Copyright © 1964 Publicaciones "El Escudo."
 Setting: From *Songs of God's Love*. Copyright © 1984 Concordia Publishing House.

Our Church Family
 Text, tune, and setting: From *The Little Christian's Songbook*. Copyright © 1975 Concordia Publishing House.

Our Hands We Fold
 Tune and setting: From *A Child's Garden of Song*. Copyright © 1949 Concordia Publishing House.

Praise God, from Whom All Blessings Flow
 Setting: From *Songs of God's Love*. Copyright © 1984 Concordia Publishing House.

Praise Him, Praise Him
 Setting: From *Songs of God's Love*. Copyright © 1984 Concordia Publishing House.

Psalm 8
 Text, tune, and setting: Copyright 1975 Graded Press. Used by permission.

Rejoice in the Lord Always
 Setting: From *Songs of God's Love*. Copyright © 1984 Concordia Publishing House.

Ring the Bells
 Text: From *Integrating the Faith,* Vol. 1, Teachers Guide. Copyright © 1986 Concordia Publishing House.

Rise and Shine (Arky, Arky)
 Setting: © 1981 Maranatha! Music. All rights reserved. International copyright secured. Used by permission.

Say to the Lord, I Love You
 Text, tune, and setting: By Ernie Rettino and Debby Kerner. © 1981 Rettino/Kerner Publishing. Admin. by Maranatha! Music. All rights reserved. International copyright secured. Used by permission.

Since My Heavenly Father
 Setting: From *Songs of God's Love*. Copyright © 1984 Concordia Publishing House.

Thank You for the World So Sweet
 Tune and setting: Copyright © 1989 Concordia Publishing House.

Thank You, Loving Father
 Text, tune, and setting: Sts. 1–4, tune, and setting from *Little Children, Sing to God!* Copyright © 1960 Concordia Publishing House. Sts. 5–6 from *The Little Christian's Songbook*. Copyright © 1975 Concordia Publishing House.

The Best Book of All
 Text, tune, and setting: Copyright by Herald Press, Scottdale, PA 15683. Reprinted by permission.

The B-I-B-L-E
 Text: © 1980 by Lillenas Publishing Co. All rights reserved. Used by permission.

The Butterfly Song
 Text, tune, and setting: By Brian Howard. © 1974, 1975 CELEBRATION. Admin. by Maranatha! Music. All rights reserved. International copyright secured. Used by permission.

The Hats Are in the Drum
 Text: From *Integrating the Faith*, Vol. 1, Teachers Guide. Copyright © 1986 Concordia Publishing House.

The King of Glory
 Text: Copyright 1966 by Willard F. Jabusch, University of St. Mary of the Lake, Mundelein Seminary, Mundelein, IL 60060. Used by permission.
 Setting: From *Joyful Sounds*. Copyright © 1977 Concordia Publishing House.

The Lord Is Good to Me (*The Johnny Appleseed Song*)
 Text, tune, and setting: By Kim Gannon and Walter Kent. © 1946 Walt Disney Music Company. Copyright Renewed. Printed by Permission. All Rights Reserved.

This Is the Day
 Text and tune: Copyright 1967, 1980 Scripture in Song. Administered by Maranatha! Music. All rights reserved. International copyright secured. Used by permission.

This Is the Feast
 Text: Copyright © 1978 *Lutheran Book of Worship*. By permission of Concordia Publishing House.
 Tune and setting: Copyright © 1975, 1988 by Richard Hillert. Used by permission.

This Is the Way We Dress for Church
 Text: From *Jesus Loves Me*, Teachers Guide. Copyright © 1985 Concordia Publishing House.

This Little Gospel Light of Mine
 Setting: From *Songs of God's Love*. Copyright © 1984 Concordia Publishing House.

Two Little Eyes
 Text: Spanish stanza from *Culto Cristiano*. Copyright © 1964 Publicaciones "El Escudo."

We Are in God's House Today
 Text and setting: From *A Child's Garden of Song*. Copyright © 1949 Concordia Publishing House.

We Are the Church
 Text, tune, and setting: Copyright © 1972 by Hope Publishing Company, Carol Stream, IL 60188. All Rights Reserved. Used by Permission.

We Love
 Tune: Copyright © 1975 by Graded Press. Used by permission.

We Pray for Each Other
 Text and tune: Copyright © 1953 O. Wm. Luecke. Used by permission.
 Setting: From *Songs of God's Love*. Copyright © 1984 Concordia Publishing House.

We Will Help the Little Children
 Text: From *Integrating the Faith*, Vol. 1, Teachers Guide. Copyright © 1986 Concordia Publishing House.

When I'm Feeling Scared or Sad
 Text, tune, and setting: © 1988 Herb Associates, 11641 Palmer Rd., Bloomington, MN 55437. Used by permission.

Where Is Jesus
 Text: From *Jesus My Friend*, Teachers Guide. Copyright © 1985 Concordia Publishing House.

Where Is Jesus? Everywhere
 Text: By Norma Voertman. Copyright © 1989 Concordia Publishing House.

Will You Pray for Me Today
 Text: From *Jesus My Friend*, Teachers Guide. Copyright © 1985 Concordia Publishing House.

Won't You Come and Sit with Me
 Text and tune: St. 1 and tune reprinted from MUSIC RESOURCE BOOK, LCA Parish Education curriculum, copyright © 1976 Lutheran Church Press. Reprinted by permission of Augsburg Fortress. Sts. 2–3 copyright © 1989 Concordia Publishing House.

Zacchaeus
 Text, tune, and setting: From *Songs for Preschool Children* © 1946. Revised edition © 1958. The Standard Publishing Company, Cincinnati, Ohio. Division of Standex International Corporation. Used by Permission.

Topical Index

Advent, 77–80
    Light one candle, Advent's here — 107

Angels
    All night, all day — 39
    Chatter with the angels soon in the morning — 20
    God has sent His angels down — 26

Animals
    If I were a butterfly — 72
    The Lord told Noah, there's gonna be a floody, floody — 66

Baptism, 97–98

Bible
    God made me, God made me — 75
    I open my Bible book and read — 54
    The best book of all is the Bible — 49
    The B-I-B-L-E — 48

Birthday
    Happy birthday to you — 29

Body Parts
    Blue, blue sky — 75
    God made me, Every part you see — 76
    I can stamp and stamp my feet — 21
    I have a hello in my heart — 10
    I have hands that will clap, clap, clap — 29
    My little hands can pat the clay — 37
    Touch your finger to your nose — 18
    Two little eyes to look to God — 36

Call to Worship
    Come and go with me to my Father's house — 99
    Happy now we gather — 9
    Our church family meets to learn God's Word — 11
    Tiptoe quietly — 8
    We are in God's house today — 12

Christmas, 81–91
    Christmas is a time of joys — 107
    Ring the bells, ring the bells — 108

Church
    I am the church — 106
    Our church family meets to learn God's Word — 11
    This is the way we dress for church — 108

Closing, 39–40

Creation, 72–76
    Every flower, soft and gay — 30
    God made all the food we eat — 71
    God made you, (name) — 102
    I can stamp and stamp my feet — 21
    My God is so great, so strong and so mighty — 64
    My little hands can pat the clay — 37
    Two little eyes to look to God — 36

Daily Living, 23–38
    God chose me and God chose you — 107
    God loves you, and I love you — 100
    God, our Father, hear Your children — 14
    Helpers, helpers, everywhere — 107
    I am the church — 106
    If you feel happy — 60
    It's good to give thanks to the Lord — 61
    Jesus loves children, Jesus loves me — 108
    Praise Him, praise Him, all you little children — 68
    The hats are in the drum — 108
    We love because God first loved us — 54
    We will help the little children — 109
    Will you be a friend of mine — 107

Emotions
    I have the joy, joy, joy, joy down in my heart — 62
    I'm as happy as can be — 25
    I'm inright, outright, upright, downright happy all the time — 59
    If you feel happy — 60
    Jesus, You help sick people, sad people, mad people — 34
    When I'm happy I remember God loves me — 38

Family
    Dear Father in heaven — 13
    Go tell your brother — 107
    I am special, I am special — 108
    Love, love, love — 30
    We pray for each other — 15

Foreign Language Songs
    Jesus loves me, this I know (*Refrain*) — 42
    Mis dos ojitos que miran a Dios — 36
    ¿Quién puede hacer las flores? — 74

Forgiveness
    Amigos de Cristo (*Refrain*) — 23
    I'm sorry, I'm sorry — 27
    When I talk to Jesus — 14

Friends
    Hello, hello! How are you — 9
    I have a friend and a good friend too — 25
    I'm glad you're you — 28
    Will you be a friend of mine — 107

God's Care
    All night, all day — 39
    Autumn, autumn, coming fast — 107
    Do you know who died for me — 93
    Every flower, soft and gay — 30
    God has sent His angels down — 26
    God is near me, God is near me — 107
    God is so good — 57
    God, our Father, hear Your children — 14
    Helpers, helpers, everywhere — 107
    He's got the whole world in His hands — 101
    I'm as happy as can be — 25
    In our work and in our play — 26
    Jesus is my special Friend — 43
    Jesus loves children, Jesus loves me — 108

Jesus loves the little children	94
Jesus said, "I'm with you."	32
When I go riding along, along	24
Where is Jesus? Where is Jesus	109
Where is Jesus? Where is Jesus? Everywhere	109

Helpers

God chose me and God chose you	107
God made me, God made me	75
Helpers, helpers, everywhere	107
I am special, I am special	108
Jesus wants me for a helper	33
The hats are in the drum	108
We will help the little children	109

Holy Week/Easter, 92–96

The King of Glory comes, the whole world rejoices (*Refrain*)	77

Jesus, 41–47

Amigos de Cristo (*Refrain*)	23
Did you hear the news	105
Do you know who died for me	93
Go tell your brother	107
God loves me dearly	85
Good morning, good morning, good morning to you	8
I am trusting you, Lord Jesus	24
I can tell	99
I love to tell the story (*Refrain*)	100
If anybody asks you who I am	98
I'm as happy as can be	25
I'm sorry, I'm sorry	27
Jesus came from heaven	92
Jesus is our friend	108
Jesus loves children, Jesus loves me	108
Jesus loves the little children	94
Jesus wants me for a helper	33
Jesus, You help sick people, sad people, mad people	34
Oh, you can't keep Jesus' love in a box	35
Someone's coming, Someone special	77
When I talk to Jesus	14
Where is Jesus? Where is Jesus	109
Where is Jesus? Where is Jesus? Everywhere	109
Will you be a friend of mine	107

Liturgy

Alleluia. Lord, to whom shall we go	48
This is the feast of victory for our God (*Refrain*)	95

Movement

Chatter with the angels soon in the morning	20
God made me, Every part you see	76
I can stamp and stamp my feet	21
I have hands that will clap, clap, clap	29
If you feel happy	60
I'm inright, outright, upright, downright happy all the time	59
In my beginning God made me so small	27
This is the way we dress for church	108
Touch your finger to your nose	18

Name Songs

God made you, (*name*)	102

Hello, everybody	7
Hello, hello! How are you	9
Jesus said, "I'm with you."	32

Offering, 22

Our hands we fold, our heads we bow	17

Opening, 7–12

Come and go with me to my Father's house	99
It's a new day, it's a new day	108
This is the day (*this is the day*)	53

Piggyback Songs, 107–109

Praise and Thanksgiving, 56–71

Alleluia. Lord, to whom shall we go	48
Did you hear the news	105
God loves me dearly	85
He's got the whole world in His hands	101
If I were a butterfly	72
I'm as happy as can be	25
It's a new day, it's a new day	108
Jesus is our friend	108
My best Friend is Jesus	45
Oh, how I love Jesus	44
Rejoice in the Lord always	52
Thank You for the world so sweet	17
The Lord is good to me	16
The Lord is great! Everybody sing	50
Touch your finger to your nose	18

Prayer, 13–15

Happy now we gather	9
Thank You, God, for Sunday school	39
Will you pray for me today	109

Prayer/Mealtime, 16–17

Refrains

All good gifts around us	71
(WE PLOW THE FIELDS AND SCATTER)	
All night, all day	39
Alleluia, alleluia	56
(A HYMN OF GLORY LET US SING)	
Amigos de Cristo	23
Hark! The herald angels sing	86
He has done marvelous things	57
(EARTH AND ALL STARS)	
I am the church	106
(WE ARE THE CHURCH)	
I love to tell the story	100
Oh, come, let us adore Him	87
(OH, COME, ALL YE FAITHFUL)	
Oh, how I love Jesus	44
(THERE IS A NAME I LOVE TO HEAR)	
On this day God gave us	87
(LET OUR GLADNESS HAVE NO END)	
The King of Glory comes, the whole world rejoices	77
This is the feast of victory for our God	95

Responses

Good morning, good morning, good morning to you	8
Hello, everybody	7

Little children, can you tell	86
This is the day (*this is the day*)	53

Scripture, 48–55

God made me, God made me	75
The Lord told Noah, there's gonna be a floody, floody	66

Self-Esteem

God chose me and God chose you	107
God made me, God made me	75
God made you, *(name)*	102
Hello, everybody	7
I am special, I am special	108
I have hands that will clap, clap, clap	29
If I were a butterfly	72
I'm glad you're you	28
In my beginning God made me so small	27
My little hands can pat the clay	37

Senses

Blue, blue sky	75
God made you, *(name)*	102
My little hands can pat the clay	37

Sickness

Jesus, You help sick people, sad people, mad people	34
We pray for each other	15

Songs for Signing

Jesus loves me, this I know	42
My best Friend is Jesus	45
Oh, how I love Jesus	44

Praise Him, praise Him, all you little children	68

Thanksgiving

All good gifts around us	71
God made all the food we eat	71
He has done marvelous things	57
It's good to give thanks to the Lord	61
Thank You for the world so sweet	17
The Lord is good to me	16

Transition

Come and go with me to my Father's house	99
Tiptoe quietly	8
Won't you come and sit with me	37

Trust

God is near me, God is near me	107
I am trusting you, Lord Jesus	24
Jesus is my special Friend	43
My God is so great, so strong and so mighty	64

Wiggles Out, 18–21

Witness, 99–106

Go tell it on the mountain	84
Go tell your brother	107
Hear us sing; News we bring	91
If anybody asks you who I am	98
Jesus loves children, Jesus loves me	108
Jesus wants me for a helper	33
We're gonna go, go tell about Jesus	104

Index of First Lines and Common Titles

Title	Page
A HYMN OF GLORY LET US SING (Refrain)	56
ADVENT SONG	107
ADVENT WREATH SONG	80
All good gifts around us	71
All night, all day	39
Alleluia, alleluia	56
Alleluia. Lord, to whom shall we go	48
Amigos de Cristo (Refrain)	23
ARKY, ARKY	66
As each happy Christmas	81
Autumn, autumn, coming fast	107
Away in a manger, no crib for a bed	83
Away in a manger, no crib for a bed (Cradle Song)	82
BAPTISM SONG	97
Blue, blue sky	75
Chatter with the angels soon in the morning	20
CHILD OF GOD	98
Christ the Lord is risen today	96
Christ the Lord is risen today; Alleluia	95
Christmas Day we will sing	89
Christmas is a time of joys	107
CHRISTMAS NEWS	91
CLOSING PRAYER	39
Come and go with me to my Father's house	99
Dear Father in heaven	13
Did you hear the news	105
Do you know who died for me	93
EARTH AND ALL STARS (Refrain)	57
Every flower, soft and gay	30
Father, bless the gifts we bring You	22
Father, I adore You	13
Four candles in a ring	80
FRIENDS	107
GATHERING SONG	8
Glory be to Jesus, Who, in perfect love	93
Glory, glory, hallelujah	56
GO TELL	104
Go tell it on the mountain	84
Go tell your brother	107
God chose me and God chose you	107
GOD GAVE ME EYES	75
God has sent His angels down	26
God is my heavenly Father	97
GOD IS NEAR	26
God is near me, God is near me	107
God is so good	57
God loves me dearly	85
God loves you, and I love you	100
God made all the food we eat	71
God made me, God made me	75
God made me, Every part you see	76
God made you, (name)	102
God, our Father, hear Your children	14
GOD'S A FATHER KIND AND TRUE	30
GOD'S CARE	24
Good morning, good morning, good morning to you	8
Good-bye, good-bye, good-bye	40
Good-bye, good-bye, To you and you and you	40
Hallelu! Hallelu! Hallelu! Hallelujah! Praise ye the Lord	58
HAPPY ALL THE TIME	59
HAPPY BIRTHDAY, JESUS	88
HAPPY BIRTHDAY, LORD	89
Happy birthday to you	29
Happy day! Let us sing	92
Happy now we gather	9
Hark! The herald angels sing (Refrain)	86
He has done marvelous things	57
Hear us sing; News we bring	91
Hello, everybody	7
Hello, hello, hello	40
Hello, hello! How are you	9
Helpers, helpers, everywhere	107
He's got the whole world in His hands	101
Hosanna! Hosanna	94
I AM SORRY, JESUS	14
I am special, I am special	108
I am the church	106
I am trusting you, Lord Jesus	24
I can stamp and stamp my feet	21
I can tell	99
I have a friend and a good friend too	25
I have a hello in my heart	10
I have hands that will clap, clap, clap	29
I have the joy, joy, joy, joy down in my heart	62
I like to be in Sunday school	11
I love to tell the story (Refrain)	100
I open my Bible book and read	54
I was baptized, happy day	97
If anybody asks you who I am	98
If I were a butterfly	72
If you feel happy	60
I'm as happy as can be	25
I'm glad you're you	28
I'M GROWING	27
I'm inright, outright, upright, downright happy all the time	59
I'm sorry, I'm sorry	27
I'M WITH YOU	32
In a little stable	81
In my beginning God made me so small	27
In our work and in our play	26
It's a new day, it's a new day	108
It's good to give thanks to the Lord	61
Jesus came from heaven	92
Jesus Christ is risen today	96
Jesus is my special Friend	43
Jesus is our friend	108

Jesus listens when I pray	15
Jesus loves children, Jesus loves me	108
Jesus loves me, this I know	42
Jesus loves the little children	94
Jesus loves the little ones like me, me, me	41
JESUS, OUR GOOD FRIEND	77
Jesus said, "I'm with you."	32
Jesus wants me for a helper	33
Jesus! what a name to know	47
Jesus, You help sick people, sad people, mad people	34
LET OUR GLADNESS HAVE NO END (Refrain)	87
LET US SING FOR JOY	105
Light one candle, Advent's here	107
Light one candle for hope	78
Little children, can you tell	86
LOVE IN A BOX	35
Love, love, love	30
Making melody in my heart	63
Mary had a baby	90
Mis dos ojitos que miran a Dios	36
My best Friend is Jesus	45
MY BIBLE BOOK	54
My God is so great, so strong and so mighty	64
MY HANDS AND FEET	37
My little hands can pat the clay	37
OH, COME, ALL YE FAITHFUL (Refrain)	87
Oh, come, let us adore Him	87
Oh, how I love Jesus	44
Oh, who can make a flower	74
Oh, you can't keep Jesus' love in a box	35
On this day God gave us	87
On this happy Christmas Day	88
Our church family meets to learn God's Word	11
Our hands we fold, our heads we bow	17
Praise God, from whom all blessings flow	65
Praise Him, praise Him, all you little children	68
PSALM 8	50
¿Quién puede hacer las flores?	74
Rejoice in the Lord always	52
Ring the bells, ring the bells	108
RISE AND SHINE	66
SAY TO THE LORD, I LOVE YOU	18
Since my heavenly Father	22
Someone's coming, Someone special	77
Thank You for the world so sweet	17
Thank You, God, for Sunday school	39
THANK YOU, LOVING FATHER	71
The best book of all is the Bible	49
The B-I-B-L-E	48
THE BUTTERFLY SONG	72
The hats are in the drum	108
THE JOHNNY APPLESEED SONG	16
The King of Glory comes, the whole world rejoices (Refrain)	77
The Lord is good to me	16
The Lord is great! Everybody sing	50
The Lord told Noah, there's gonna be a floody, floody	66
THERE IS A NAME I LOVE TO HEAR (Refrain)	44
This is the day (this is the day)	53
This is the feast of victory for our God (Refrain)	95
This is the way we dress for church	108
This little Gospel light of mine	103
Tiptoe quietly	8
Touch your finger to your nose	18
Two little eyes to look to God	36
We are in God's house today	12
WE ARE THE CHURCH (Refrain)	106
We love because God first loved us	54
WE PLOW THE FIELDS AND SCATTER (Refrain)	71
We pray for each other	15
We will help the little children	109
We're gonna go, go tell about Jesus	104
When I go riding along, along	24
When I talk to Jesus	14
WHEN I'M FEELING SCARED OR SAD	38
When I'm happy I remember God loves me	38
Where is Jesus? Where is Jesus	109
Where is Jesus? Where is Jesus? Everywhere	109
Who made the sky so bright and blue	74
Will you be a friend of mine	107
Will you pray for me today	109
Won't you come and sit with me	37
Zacchaeus was a wee little man	55